DATE DUE

NO 17 '99			
DE 10 '99			
OC 21 07			

DEMCO 38-296

CRIME AND THE
NEW IMMIGRANTS

CRIME AND THE NEW IMMIGRANTS

Edited by

HAROLD M. LAUNER, Ph.D.
Seton Hall University

and

JOSEPH E. PALENSKI, Ph.D.
Seton Hall University

CHARLES C THOMAS • PUBLISHER
Springfield • Illinois • U.S.A.

...ributed Throughout the World by

...THOMAS • PUBLISHER
2600 South First Street
Springfield, Illinois 62794-9265

© *1989 by* CHARLES C THOMAS • PUBLISHER

ISBN 0-398-05520-3

Library of Congress Catalog Card Number: 88-19827

With THOMAS BOOKS *careful attention is given to all details of manufacturing and design. It is the Publisher's desire to present books that are satisfactory as to their physical qualities and artistic possibilities and appropriate for their particular use.* THOMAS BOOKS *will be true to those laws of quality that assure a good name and good will.*

Printed in the United States of America
Q-R-3

Library of Congress Cataloging in Publication Data

Crime and the new immigrants / edited by Harold M. Launer and Joseph
E. Palenski.
   p. cm.
   Chiefly reprints of articles originally published 1978-1985.
   Includes bibliographies and index.
   Contents: Introduction / Harold M. Launer and Joseph E. Palenski -
- Policing the new immigrant ghettos / Philip B. Taft, Jr. --
Chinatown / Rob Wilson -- The Vietnamese crime network / Greg Gross
-- Chinatown's immigrant gangs / Delbert Joe and Norman Robinson --
Isolation and stigmatization in the development of an underclass :
the case of Chicano gangs in East Los Angeles / Joan W. Moore -- The
Chicano and the law : an analysis of community-police conflict in an
urban barrio / Alfredo Mirandé -- On the structure of ethnic crime
in America / Kenneth L. Wilson and W. Allen Martin -- Survivors &
connivers : the adaptation of extra-legal behavior by new Russian
immigrants / Lydia S. Rosner.
   ISBN 0-398-05520-3
   1. Crime and criminals--United States--Case studies.
2. Immigrants--United States--Case studies. I. Launer, Harold M.
II. Palenski, Joseph E.
HV6181.C75   1988
364'.973--dc19
                                                    88-19827
                                                    CIP

CONTRIBUTORS

GREG GROSS

Contributing Writer
The National Centurion

DELBERT JOE

School Counsellor
Vancouver School District

HAROLD M. LAUNER

Assistant Professor of
Anthropology and Criminal Justice
Seton Hall University

W. ALLEN MARTIN

Associate Professor of Sociology
University of Texas, Tyler

ALFREDO MIRANDÉ

Professor of Sociology
University of California, Riverside

JOAN W. MOORE

Professor of Sociology
University of Wisconsin, Milwaukee

JOSEPH E. PALENSKI

Associate Professor of Sociology
and Criminal Justice
Seton Hall University

NORMAN ROBINSON

Professor of Educational Administration
Simon Fraser University

Crime and the New Immigrants

LYDIA S. ROSNER

Assistant Professor of Sociology
John Jay College of Criminal Justice

PHILIP B. TAFT, JR.

Contributing Editor
Police Magazine

KENNETH L. WILSON

Associate Professor of Sociology
Florida Atlantic University

ROB WILSON

Contributing Writer
Police Magazine

This work is dedicated to our grandparents

PREFACE

SINCE 1965, the American system of justice has undergone severe scrutiny. During the sixties and seventies major demographic shifts in our nation's population, a revival among Black Americans seeking equal protection, and changing attitudes towards women's roles served to test the meaning of civil rights. As a result, federal legislation, prompted by numerous test cases brought before our courts, resulted in accommodation and change by criminal justice policymakers at all levels.

When we compare the decade of the eighties to that of the previous two decades, it appears that accommodation of issues surrounding the civil rights of minority groups has diminished within our political and legal system. Yet, within this decade a new challenge has appeared to confront our society: that of dealing with new immigrant crime patterns.

While crime among newly arriving immigrants to America's shores is not unique the styles, routines, and customs of those arriving within the past twenty years appear to be different from those of previous arrivals. Equipped only with the knowledge gained through reforms of the sixties and seventies, American criminal justice policymakers are repeatedly pressed to respond to the new immigrant crime problem. Yet, public policy suffers from both a lack of fact and theory when it comes to new immigrant crime.

This book explores the new immigrant crime problem. It provides both descriptive and theoretical data on new immigrant crime activities as seen through the eyes of criminal justice practitioners and social scientists. From the descriptions given, it is hoped that the reader gains a better understanding of the cultural life-styles of our new arrivals. In the process,we hope that a greater effort is made by both policymakers and practitioners to pay more attention to "due process" problems that affect the liberty and well-being of new immigrants. Only by rededicating ourselves to issues surrounding basic freedoms can the reforms of the sixties and seventies become the foundation for meaningful change in the present and future.

Harold M. Launer
Joseph E. Palenski

Sociology/Anthropology Department
Seton Hall University
South Orange, New Jersey 07079

REPRINT ACKNOWLEDGMENTS

THE VIETNAMESE CRIME NETWORK

Greg Gross

Reprinted from:
The National Centurion, Vol. 1, No. 8, Pages 23-28, 1983

CHINATOWN'S IMMIGRANT GANGS: THE NEW YOUNG WARRIOR CLASS

Delbert Joe and Norman Robinson

Reprinted from:
Criminology, Vol. 18, No. 3, Pages 337-345, 1980

THE CHICANO AND THE LAW: AN ANALYSIS OF COMMUNITY-POLICE CONFLICT IN AN URBAN BARRIO

Alfredo Mirandé

Reprinted from:
Pacific Sociological Review, Vol. 24, No. 1, Pages 65-86, 1981

ISOLATION AND STIGMATIZATION IN THE DEVELOPMENT OF AN UNDERCLASS: THE CASE OF CHICANO GANGS IN EAST LOS ANGELES

Joan W. Moore

Reprinted from:
Social Problems, Vol. 33, No. 1, Pages 1-12, 1985

POLICING THE NEW IMMIGRANT GHETTOS

Philip B. Taft, Jr.

Reprinted from:
Police Magazine, Vol. 5, No. 4, Pages 10-26, 1982

CHINATOWN: NO LONGER A COZY ASSIGNMENT
Rob Wilson

Reprinted from:
Police Magazine, Pages 18-29, July, 1978

INTRODUCTION

THIS BOOK is devoted to the topic of New Immigrant Crime in America. The concept of "New Immigrant Crime" conveys the notion that today's newly arriving immigrant groups are distinct from their earlier arriving counterparts. Dramatic events, like those portrayed in the 1987 seizing of the Atlanta Federal Penitentiary by Cuban inmates, magnify the fact that today's immigrant crime question is a complicated matter. Unlike the patterns of years past, today's immigrants are highly varied with respect to national origin, economic predicament, and circumstances which have driven them to America's shores.

Today's new immigrants are by no means the poor and huddled masses of the past, nor are many arriving immigrant groups totally ignorant of the social settings of their adopted country. Therefore, in analyzing the crimes of new immigrants, and possible official reactions, we must pay particular attention to the social and cultural features of associated immigrant groups. More importantly, from a social science perspective, we must be careful not to impute the conventional paradigms and understandings of the past in order to comprehend the patterns of criminal behavior in America's new arrivals.

In the process of developing this text, it was quite surprising to be confronted by such a paucity of data on the topic of new immigrant crime. When we consider that the past twenty years has witnessed a vast explosion in criminal justice research and writing, and this same twenty-year period corresponds to the arrival of this new immigrant class, we might suppose a great deal of available information. Unfortunately, this is not the case.

We could present several possible reasons why such limited writings exist. However, any given reason might be criticized as conjectural and conflict with the threefold objections of this book which are as follows: **First,** to provide a descriptive and comparative base from which to interpret new immigrant crime. **Second,** to give some accounting of how existing law enforcement agents and agencies perceive and respond to new immigrant crime problems; and **third,** to fill a very serious and obvious void with respect to how new immigrant crime patterns differ from those of previous arrivals, and what such differences mean to criminal justice practitioners.

In the process of approaching the subject of new immigrant crime, we must caution readers that the present work is primarily descriptive in nature. The primary goal is to sensitize the reader to the styles and features of new immigrant crime that are affecting our society and its criminal justice system. In this respect, we wish to point out that this text is influenced by four postulates that may be used as guides for comprehension. As articulated below, each of these postulates are important for understanding why and how the new immigrant crime question is a unique problem in American criminal justice, and a problem worthy of further research and debate.

Postulate 1. Today's immigration crime question is often confused with the very different question of illegal immigration to the United States.

Postulate 2. Recent immigration to America includes nationalities whose members are familiar with complex bureaucratic structures. Therefore, in some cases new arrivals to America may be said to be **bureaucratically smart.** This fact makes it difficult to apply the knowledge gained from previous immigrations to the United States.

Postulate 3. Several new immigrant arrival groups are already represented by ethnic groups and communities that were created by previous immigrations (i.e. Cubans and Chinese). This creates problems of national and cultural identity within ethnic communities, and serves to confuse public policy concerning new immigrant behavior and crime control.

Postulate 4. The New Immigrant Crime question is hampered by the "assembly-line" approach to criminal justice which is so prevalent in American urban centers. This approach stresses speed and efficiency within the criminal justice system. Considering the fact that most new immigrants live in urban environments, it is not surprising that the "assembly-line" approach makes our criminal justice system insensitive to the cultural and linguistic backgrounds of new immigrant populations. This problem leads to prominent issues relating to civil rights and "due process" for our recent arrivals.

To orient the reader to a better understanding of the issues relating to new immigrant crime, this book has been divided into three sections.

Section I focuses on the everyday aspects of new immigrant crime from the perspective of law enforcement and social science policy-makers. The articles included attempt to describe the types of behavioral activities which makes the new immigrant crime problem unique.

Section II presents a series of case studies devoted to the development of multiple analytical frameworks for interpreting new immigrant crime activities. Studies presented include those of Chinese and Mexican-American communities.

Section III presents two articles that provide a first step towards a theoretical understanding of new immigrant crime patterns. The authors of these articles explore the utility of earlier conceptualizations of immigration and crime, for explaining the criminal behavior of recent immigrants.

Conclusion

Considering the exploratory nature of this volume, the editors wish to call for a major research and theoretical commitment by American social scientists and criminal justice specialists towards the subject of new immigrant crime. We cannot assume that our old ideas and expectations about immigrants and the process of immigration apply to today's arrivals. Therefore, our criminal justice system must develop a posture of flexibility and seek to develop new organizational structures and procedures for dealing with new immigrant crime. Failure to do so will only create a situation where both public safety and individual freedom are threatened.

CONTENTS

Section III — THEORETICAL IMPLICATIONS

CRIME AND THE
NEW IMMIGRANTS

Section I

OBSERVATIONS

CHAPTER 1

POLICING THE NEW IMMIGRANT GHETTOS

PHILIP B. TAFT, JR.

"EL CHOCO MICARRO!" ("He hit my car!") shouted the man, a Cuban refugee from the 1980 Freedom Flotilla, pointing his finger at another man, an Orthodox Jew newly arrived from Russia. The Russian stands quietly with his wife by his dented automobile. "I do not see him," he says in halting English.

Miami Beach Police Officer Rick Mendoza, a blond-haired man of Irish and Spanish descent, studies the situation. "Habla usted Ingles?" ("Do you speak English?") he asks the Cuban, who shakes his head. Mendoza tries to explain his interpretation of the accident, in which the Cuban man appears to have backed his vehicle in front of the other man's, but his Spanish is as imperfect as the Russian's English.

By this time a crowd, mostly Cuban, has gathered. A teenage girl offers her services as a translator. "Explain to him that the damage is very minor," says Mendoza, "and more than likely I am going to charge him with the accident."

The girl offers her translation and the crowd grows restless. A few of them shout in Spanish at Mendoza, pointing to the cars and trying to convince him that he is wrong. Frustrated, Mendoza turns his back to the crowd and begins to talk to the translator again. With that, a tall mustachioed man in the crowd mutters under his breath, "Que lastima que el no habla Espanol" ("What a pity that he doesn't speak Spanish").

Mendoza understands this much Spanish. "Estamos en America! Yo no necesito Espanol!" ("We are in America! I do not need Spanish!"), he snaps, his face reddening. Some of the Cubans laugh; others shake their heads and walk away.

5

"They are offended," explains the translator.

"You tell them I am offended because they don't speak English," Mendoza tells her, perfuntorily writing a summons before he leaves.

In the patrol car, Mendoza sighs as he puts his clipboard away. "Every day we get more and more of those kinds of calls. It's becoming a regular thing."

Mendoza could have been speaking for thousands of police officers all over the country. Almost five million refugees, illegal aliens and immigrants have poured into the United States over the past decade, settling everywhere from urban ghettos to rural villages. This is a significant increase over the levels of the 1960s, but more importantly, the "new immigrants" introduced several cultures that had not been represented before in the American melting pot. Thriving neighborhoods of Laotians, Cambodians, and South Vietnamese are now scattered all over California, Texas, Minnesota and Louisiana, the result of the post-1975 influx of more than 500,000 Southeast Asians. Some 100,000 Soviet Jews now call New York, Los Angeles and Miami home. Close to 50,000 Haitians have come in rickety boats from their island home. In the most dramatic exodus, 120,000 "Mariels" — so named for the Cuban port from which they embarked—came in the 1980 Freedom Flotilla. There are hundreds of thousands of South Americans in major cities. And the biggest influx continues to be the hundreds of thousands—some experts say millions—of illegal Mexican aliens who continue to stream across the border states.

The presence of these new immigrants raises a host of problems, both in practice and in theory, for the American police. The street patrol officer and investigator are confronted with alien languages and bewildering customs; some particularly vicious and cunning criminals have sprung from these communities, and the victims often refuse to cooperate with the police. In Miami, the police and the public are convinced that a few thousand hardened criminals sent by Castro from Cuban prisons in the Freedom Flotilla are responsible for a huge increase in violent crime, although some experts question this. In the face of these developments, chiefs and senior police officials must decide how best to use their limited resources in providing police services to the new cultures, investigating crime or educating officers in the new languages and customs.

Although some departments stand unyielding in the face of such challenges, others have made adjustments to the growth of the new immigrants within their jurisdictions. Dozens of departments have hired translators and added language courses to their in-service training programs. Last year, the Miami Police Department started a program of street sweeps, sending a wave of officers in cars and on foot through high-crime areas to arrest suspicious people (Mariels) on minor charges such as loitering. New York has designated four detectives or a "Cuban task force" to keep track of refugee criminals in the Bronx, Manhattan and New Jersey. The New York Police Department has also assigned its one officer who is fluent in Russian to foot patrol in the Soviet Jewish community in Brooklyn's Brighton Beach area. The Los Angeles Police Department opened a reporting center to try to open up communication with that city's booming Koreatown.

But the recession, tight budgets and a growing national disaffection for minorities and "aliens" may put an end to many of those kinds of efforts. In some regions it already has. Some police chiefs have turned to private funds to hire interpreters and produce cultural awareness seminars. Meanwhile, as the melting pot simmers and money grows more scarce, some observers are predicting racially motivated violence and an increase in mental health problems in the new immigrant ghettos.

Most chiefs and senior police officials agree that departments must make some changes in order to function among the new immigrants; but beyond that, there is debate over the police's obligation to educate the newest Americans in law, order and police procedure. Some feel that police role ends with providing standard services; others argue that the police must go far beyond that basic role and help build community morale.

The rank and file, however, take little interest in such affairs. With the exception of officers who take personal interest in the new cultures, most of them are lost when confronted with both the language and cultural barriers on the street. They complain that refugees are difficult and distant, and often complain that they're playing nursemaid to new arrivals rather than keeping the peace and catching criminals. "And no one likes that," says Santa Ana (CA) Officer James McDonald, who works the 20,000-resident Southeast Asian ghetto there. "A cop doesn't want to be a baby-sitter, he wants to be the enforcement arm of the law." As a result, both performance and morale can be damaged. "Most of them just shake their heads and walk away," says Officer Gary Felt, who works closely with one Southeast Asian community in Bellevue,

Washington. "It's more of a hassle to write a ticket. So you just walk away."

Yet for the past hundred years, the police have played a vital role in the assimilation of every new immigrant group that has come to America. And while the languages and traditions of immigrants in 1981 may be different from those of a century ago, the police role remains essentially the same: They continue to be the primary caretakers of these newest Americans. "Who else is going to do it?" asks Officer P. J. Allen in Santa Ana. "The schoolteachers are going to teach them, the doctors are going to give them shots. But who is going to take the first step forward and help these people? The police?"

Historically, police have had an immediate, intimate relationship with immigrants. The cops ambling the beat through the Jewish tenements in New York's Lower East Side or the shops in San Francisco's Chinatown were the first symbols of government for the new arrivals. While they enforced a set of laws that were strange to the immigrants and sometimes biased against them, the police also served as superintendents of the community, answering questions and smoothing out conflicts that arose from misunderstandings about American culture.

Police today remain the most accessible representatives of government for immigrant groups; they still serve as guardians, correcting inappropriate behavior and informally educating the newcomers about law and order. Yet, some important differences now exist between law enforcement in the Lower East Side in the 1920s, for example, and the East New Orleans Vietnamese district in 1982.

The police have changed. For one thing, modern peace officers no longer see themselves primarily as enforcers of community standards or caretakers of community ills; they want to be action-oriented crime fighters. While police officers once made daily rounds on foot, making personal contact with the newest ethnic groups, they now remotely observe immigrant behavior through the windows of air-conditioned patrol cars.

The distance is both real and psychological, exacerbated by a national mood of anxiety as America reexamines its "melting pot" legacy in economically uncertain times. "A lot of the cops were upset," said one Orange County, California refugee worker, recalling a 1980 cultural awareness seminar on Southeast Asians organized for local police. "They'd say, 'How come these people can get low interest loans and I can't? How come my wife is entering the job market and you can't help her?'"

The immigrants have changed as well. While many of the millions of Europeans and Asians who came to America at the turn of the century came to seek relief from political and religious oppression, their primary motive was economic. They wanted to better their lives, and they were welcomed by industries which often paid their way. Academics who study immigration patterns have noted that prior to the establishment of immigrant quotas in 1924, the number of new arrivals fluctuated with the health of the American economy.

Today, there are new immigrants who have come for the same reasons. Haitians, for example, crowded flimsy boats to escape the poorest country in the hemisphere. But immigration law admits only political refugees, not economic ones. For most of the new immigrants who have arrived legally, their primary motivation has been to flee some of the most heinous religious, political and ethnic persecution of recent times. For many of the Cambodians who have settled around the country, the choice was either escape or face execution at the hands of the Pol Pot regime. Castro proudly announced that he was "flushing his toilets" when he ordered the exodus of 120,000 "undesirables" in the 1980 Freedom Flotilla. "Most of what causes refugees to come here in the twentieth century is much, much grimmer than what motivated them to come in the nineteenth century," says Mel Lehman, information officer with Church World Service in New York.

More important, these new Americans bring with them a different view of the police, an attitude that has developed from years of watching state-controlled thugs apply brutal sanctions in the name of law and order. "They have an inherent fear and distrust of the police," says Santa Ana Lieutenant Jack Bassett. "It's an attitude that's based on old country values."

Thus, instead of a reasonable peace, a mutual distrust and suspicion separate officer and ethnic community. It is in this context that the American police and the new immigrant meet.

"Now imagine this," says the Santa Ana officer, describing a call he answered in the Southeast Asian neighborhood there. "You roll up to the apartment and you find a dead Lao man, an hysterical 80-year old Lao woman, two incensed boys who have something to do with it, and a whole shitload of onlookers. And they're all going, 'Ding-dong lang-lang! Ding-dong lang-lang!' And you can't understand a fucking thing they're saying. What the hell do you do?" He shrugs his shoulders and laughs, "I don't know."

Of all the problems faced by the officer patrolling the new immigrant ghettos, the language barrier is the most common and the most formidable. "It's the important issue," says Gary Felt. "It has to be the most frustrating thing for the patrol officer. Everything else falls into place if you are able to understand one another."

And, of course, policing falls apart at every level when communication is fractured. "Let's say I stop a Vietnamese guy," says Corporal Ken Grominsky of the Santa Ana department. "If I can't even tell him to give me his license on a simple traffic stop, then how in hell am I going to tell him what he did wrong? And if he responds, how the hell do I know if he's saying, 'Fuck you, I've got a gun,' or 'This is my last name'?"

Police in Miami Beach are familiar with the same dilemma. Thousands of Mariel refugees have settled into the seamy South Beach area, sending the crime rate soaring, police say. "See that guy?" says Lieutenant William Lamb, chief of night shift detectives, nodding to another investigator interviewing a refugee with the help of an interpreter. "He's one of my best detectives. He's cleared more homicides and locked up more people than anyone else. He's unable to interview that man. You lose a lot of the impact of surprise, a lot of your knowledge, a lot of your years of experience working through an interpreter."

Every department that must communicate with new ethnic groups has experimented with some sort of solution to the language predicament. St. Paul, Minnesota police now have 24-hour access to Hmong interpreters, to work with the 10,000 Laotian hill people who have settled there. In Seattle, crime prevention pamphlets come in seven different languages. Officers at the Wilshire division of the Los Angeles Police Department can take a basic Korean course, on duty time, to help them in their work within the burgeoning Korean population there.

None of these solutions have proven completely satisfactory. As Lamb discovered, interpreters slow down and often confuse the arrest and investigation process. Bilingual officers are a beleaguered minority on every force, often spending complete shifts racing from call to call in order to translate. "Sometimes I think that's all I do around here," says Mary Gorra, one of the Hialeah (FL) Police Department's few bilingual officers. (Gorra's task is especially taxing: Hialeah is almost 75 percent Hispanic.)

Almost every department has tried the most popular approach: simple language training for officers. But the effectiveness of those short courses, usually administered on limited budgets, is a matter of debate among officers and administrators.

"Crash courses are a waste of time," says Stephen Hrehus, Brighton Beach's Russian-speaking officer, who learned his Russian as a child. "It's like college Spanish. All I remember from my college Spanish is, 'Las montarias en Mexico son bonitas'—the mountains in Mexico are pretty. All that in six weeks! In six weeks, you are not going to be able to learn much of anything."

Others disagree, "You should learn basic phrases, like: 'Put your hands up!,' or 'Don't move,!' " says Art Placencia, one of two Los Angeles officers who man the Koreatown Police-Community Center, a storefront operation that was opened to encourage crime reporting in that neighborhood. "What if you got a situation where you say, 'Freeze!' and he doesn't freeze and then he gets shot?" That very situation arose in New York City in July 1980, when two patrol officers answered a call to a Brooklyn supermarket. From inside the store, a Korean man holding a gun shouted something to the officers, neither of whom spoke Korean, and they shot him dead. The man turned out to be a security guard, a newly arrived immigrant who had just found a job. A grand jury did not indict the officers involved.

Compounding the language problems are cultural gaps that can make police work among new immigrants tedious, unnerving, or even dangerous. Frequently, officers feel like parents explaining social customs to small children. "Those fences are where the Southeast Asians hang out their squid to dry," explains Officer James McDonald, driving through the refugee-packed Volatire apartment complex in Santa Ana. "You try and tell them, 'Okay, take those thousands of squid down from the fence because they're a health hazard.' Well, that's a real problem. Those are the kind of cultural jobs that can be a bother."

More often, the officer must make legal judgments that are complicated by custom and tradition. In Miami, Mariels continue, in Havana tradition, arguing politics on the street corner; police there must decide whether a frenzied gathering is a political convocation or an assault. "I'm concerned that the police just don't pick up anyone off the street," said one prosecutor there. Many Indochinese parents practice "coin rubbing," a medicinal technique in which coins are scraped against a child's neck to drive away evil spirits. Sometimes teachers or nurses see the marks and call the police. "It sure looks like child abuse, and it is, by our standards," says Major Noreen Skagen of the Seattle Police Department. "But for them, it's folk medicine."

Unless an officer is made aware of the customs of a particular culture, an innocent encounter can be misinterpreted. It is not odd for

Vietnamese drivers to leave their cars when pulled over for traffic violations so they can bow in order to show the officer respect. Police who work in Korean communities are warned that handing a ticket or summons to a Korean with one hand instead of two can be interpreted as a sign of disrespect. In Hispanic communities in Miami and New York, juvenile officers are told not to be insulted if a Cuban youth looks down when facing police: It is a sign of deference to elders.

Sometimes, the cultural differences can produce volatile situations. When Los Angeles police made felony arrests of Southeast Asians, suspects frequently would flee or become overly anxious, causing police to consider drawing their weapons. Later, police discovered that the arrest position — kneeling, back turned to the officer, hands clasped behind the head — recalled the position used for executions performed by police in Vietnam. "You've got to be careful of those things," says Bellevue's Gary Felt, who once worked in Santa Ana. "We warned officers [in Santa Ana] that the suspect may decide to fight for his very life, because that's what he's thinking: He's about to lose his head."

Several departments have taken major steps to overcome the cultural differences that impeded police work. The Los Angeles Police Department opened its first storefront reporting station in Koreatown after that community filled with new immigrants. In perhaps the most enthusiastic effort by any group of law enforcement agencies, several Orange County departments joined together and produced a series of instructional videotapes, for both officers and immigrants, and convened a series of seminars to explain Southeast Asian culture. Among the leaders in this Task Force on Police-Asian Relations (TOPAR) is the Santa Ana force.

While those efforts are extolled by community relations departments and lauded by chiefs in speeches, they often have little real effect on the relationship between the officers and the new immigrants. Many officers in Koreatown, for example, complain loud and long about the residents' unwillingness to learn English. "My feeling is that they are in America. They should learn English," said one sergeant, echoing the sentiments of most of his peers. "If I was in Germany, I'd have to learn German, right?" Police officials in San Diego learned an important lesson about assimilation when they set up a crime prevention conference for Southeast Asian refugees. Thousands of leaflets were printed and several translators brought in. No one showed up. "The Vietnamese culture wouldn't have taken this as something to respond to," commented one refugee worker. "If the police want anything, they are going to have to be aggressive about it. If they don't keep coming to them, the Vietnamese won't open up."

In dealing with Vietnamese, the legacy of the Vietnam War sometimes comes into play. One Santa Ana officer, a war veteran, was asked how he would get Vietnamese suspects out of a house: "He said, 'I should do like I did in Vietnam—throw a hand grenade in,' " recalled Santa Ana Chief Raymond Davis. "That kind of thing disturbs me. The adjustment of the Vietnam veteran is one of the biggest concerns."

Most other chiefs and senior officials, however, say the presence of Vietnam War veterans in Southeast Asian ghettos doesn't worry them. They reason that if a veteran has passed police psychological tests, his mental health is sound. The half-dozen Vietnam veterans interviewed by *Police Magazine* agree. "Anyone who gives you that kind of stuff about flashbacks and problems is full of crap," says James McDonald, a Navy veteran. "You went to Vietnam because you were told; you do this because you are told." Several of these officers confessed to moments of confusion and doubt when patrolling the Southeast Asian neighborhoods, but they said they had resolved their wartime experiences long ago. As Mike Walker, an officer with the Garden Grove, California department said, "I'm not fighting the Vietnam War anymore." Indeed, some observers say that because of their overseas experience, psychological struggles and maturity, Vietnam veterans often are better suited to police new ethnic communities than many of their less experienced counterparts.

In some instances, an insensitivity tinged with racism infects police attitudes. In Miami, for instance, Chief Kenneth Harms proudly observed that the department's cultural awareness conferences on Cubans and Haitians were "designed to acquaint officers with other cultures and make them more sensitive to traditions...and the diversity of cultures in Miami." When asked about the effect of one of those seminars, one officer responded, "It was a joke. We sat around with a couple of shrinkheads who told us that the Haitians were oppressed people. Well, I don't give a damn. What the hell does that have to do with me? They still aren't welcome in my house."

Some observers feel that this kind of intolerance may be the result of frustration more than prejudice. "You have to understand that cops are very competitive," explains John Clark, a Korean who works with Los

Angeles Police Department's Asian Task Force, a group of eleven officers who handle only Asian-related police problems. "When they confront a barrier and they can't overcome it, it's frustrating. They get angry. That's what the culture and language barriers do. They breed frustration, which breeds stereotypes."

"It's very frustrating," agrees officer Earl Graham, an administrative assistant with the Westminster (CA) Police Department in Orange County. "Officers are people. Our reaction is, 'Why do we have to go to another language? Why do we have to print the motor vehicle book in Vietnamese? Why are we catering to them?' But then the answer is obvious: We've never had a culture come to us like this." Graham sighs. "Changing times! I don't know what police can do except go with the flow."

Many officers, however, have another way of relieving the frustration. "Unless it's a major incident, 99 out of 100 times we'll say, 'Aw, fuck it,'" confided one Santa Ana officer. "It's just one more problem. And I could do without one more problem."

The involvement of immigrant groups in serious crime appears, at least on the surface, to be minimal, with the exception of Cuban Mariels. Most officers who patrol immigrant communities say they are extraordinarily quiet. "We probably have fewer problems coming from that area than anywhere else," says officer Jimmy Adams, who works closely with the Vietnamese population in East New Orleans.

Few departments keep separate statistics based on ethnic groups; those that do say the figures show little criminal activity on the part of the new immigrants. In 1980 in Santa Ana, only 84 Southeast Asians were arrested, eight for felony offenses. Police are more certain that the greatest crime problem in these new communities arises from within the culture itself.

Some departments report an increasing number of calls to settle domestic disputes. In Los Angeles's Koreatown, police say that marital battles are on the rise as wives take on jobs and leave the home, threatening the traditional Korean husband's fierce pride as the sole breadwinner. "It's bad," says Sargeant Kip Meyerhoff, who is fluent in Korean, "and it's getting worse every day." Several Hialeah officers say that family disputes have skyrocketed since the arrival of thousands of Mariels. "We have a great number of domestics," says Officer Mary Gorra. "Cubans are very hotheaded. They are very good for disturbances and fights."

In most Southeast Asian communities, however, police say there are few family disturbances. Despite media attention given to several refugee suicides, none of the police departments contacted by *Police Magazine* reported any rash of suicides among refugees and immigrants.

There are also mixed reports about victimization among new ethnic communities. Captain John Kleghorn, one of the commanding officers at the Wilshire division station in Los Angeles, says that "95 percent of crime in Koreatown is done by outsiders. The main thing that is attractive is the geographical location. Hispanic and Black suspects can get in and out very rapidly. The incidents when you meet a Korean suspect are very rare." In St. Paul, Chief McCutcheon says that Hmongs have become favorite targets for angry gangs. In several instances, both black and white gangs have joined forces to fight the Hmongs. "We really have a cultural revolution going on, and it's brought the blacks and whites together, resisting the intrusion of the Hmongs," McCutcheon says.

Some police officials believe that immigrant crime statistics and calls for service are artificially low. As Westminster's Officer Graham puts it: "There seems to be a reluctance to report crime." Many officials say they sense a substantial degree of criminal activity and social problems among the immigrants and refugees that never come to the attention of police. Some of this is attributable to language problems and feelings of powerlessness. Police also say that among Asian populations many victims are unwilling to report embarrassing crimes for fear of losing face.

The biggest factor in keeping immigrants from calling the police, however, is usually fear—both fear of the police and of each other. Among illegal immigrants, victims are afraid of calling the police because they fear deportation. Even legal immigrants are often afraid of the police, because they come from countries where repressive regimes mete out discipline and punishment through the police. "They don't come forward at all," says Officer Barry Brisacone, describing the Russian population in Brighton Beach. "I think they are scared because of what they faced in Russia. You really don't speak with the Russians. They're afraid of us."

For the 21,000 Haitians who are estimated to have settled in Miami, the word "police" means torture, even death. In Haiti, autocrat "Baby Doc" Duvalier exercises his rigid control through the Tonton Macoute (literally, "Uncle Bagmen" in Creole), his 10,000-strong secret police. The terrifying presence of the Macoute is still felt, in absentia, among the refugees. "They don't follow-up with the police, because they feel threatened," says Reverend Gerard Jean-Juste, executive director of the

Haitian Refugee Center in Miami. "They feel that if you go after the offender, he might have contacts in Haiti and the Macoute will get your parents."

America's newest immigrants also fear retaliatory violence from members of their own community, a factor that keeps crime statistics low. Gangs and loosely organized criminal rings execute reprisals when extortion fees go unpaid or witnesses cooperate with the police. "The retaliation in Southeast Asia was very, very real and very, very brutal," says Gary Felt. That was evident in 1980 in Irvine, California, when four Vietnamese, allegedly gang members, stormed into a manufacturing plant and, in front of 60 other Southeast Asians, attacked a Vietnamese man with machetes, inflicting wounds on his arms. Although the investigation is still open, police suspect it as related to extortion. "And that's why the crime isn't solved," says Felt. "Sixty people saw it happen and none of them wanted to get involved because they feared the same thing would happen to them."

To maintain order and enforce justice, many of the new immigrant communities have continued to rely on informal practices from their old countries. In Koreatown, a victim may demand restitution from the family of an offender, and the father of that family is obligated to comply lest he lose face. Rarely are police informed of such solutions. "They call us all hot and bothered and tell us they want to have this guy go to jail," says John Byun, a Korean officer who serves on the Asian Task Force. "When we ask them to make a report, they have already been contacted by the perpetrator's family or the perpetrator himself. To us, that's difficult and frustrating." In Brighton Beach, a board of elders quietly ensures community equilibrium. "They handle certain things in the community and take care of things by themselves," says Stephen Hrehus. "It's there, and the police aren't supposed to know anything about it. But we do."

A classic example of the difficulties of breaking through the wall of suspicion separating immigrants from the police can be found in Los Angeles. Fleeing the economic and political turmoil of their homeland, more that 100,000 South Koreans settled there between 1975 and 1980. They earned a reputation for hard work, and by 1981, Koreatown had become the largest and most affluent Oriental community in Los Angeles, eclipsing substantial Chinese and Japanese neighborhoods. Calls to the police were rare. On the surface, it seemed an example of how industriousness could overcome cultural handicaps.

But in June of that year, an investigative article published in the *Los Angeles Times* exposed the darker side of Koreatown. Merchants and law enforcement officials admitted that Koreatown was riddled with extortion, protection rackets, and loansharking; gangs roamed Eighth Street, the heart of the community; and burglaries and violent assaults, executed by both Koreans and outsiders, were on the rise. But the police were never called.

Following the *Times* article, the LAPD arranged for Korean language courses to be offered to officers who patrolled Koreatown. Assisted with funds from the Korean business community, the department also opened the Koreantown Police-Community Center in the heart of the community. This small reporting center is staffed by two officers and an interpreter; it is open only during business hours and is not a full-fledged precinct house.

According to both parties, the center is a public relations success. But some of the gulf of silence still exists between police and the Korean community. "They just won't talk with us, " complained one sergeant. "I just got done [reporting] one robbery and the problem is that there are no victims now. They won't talk." The officers, on the other hand, "still neglect the Koreans," says John Clark of the Asia Task Force. "A lot of the cops still say, 'Shit another Korean. Let's not even file it.'"

Unlike the rank and file, chiefs and police administrators are in almost total agreement that police departments should adjust their routines and policies in order to respond to the unique needs of new ethnic communities. "We just can't sit back smugly," says St. Paul's McCutcheon. "We have to work with them. If we don't, then they withdraw and that causes us more problems than reaching out and giving them a hand."

In Santa Ana, Chief Raymond Davis agrees: "The police have an obligation to help the ethnic group get settled in the most rapid way. If you don't try to make the transition as smooth as possible, then you're in for trouble. Making it easier for a new community to settle is a good investment in the future."

There are differences of opinion, however, regarding how far police should extend themselves. Some police leaders, like Minneapolis Police Department Chief Anthony Bouza, take a broad view of police work among immigrants, one that includes "building community morale. The police have a very important societal function that goes far beyond the enforcement of the law," says Bouza. "It involves maintenance and support of the community. We have a legitimate right to anticipate them learning the language and culture. We also have to extend ourselves toward them. The pot has always been half melting and half not."

Others, however, are careful to draw boundaries for police work, establishing limits to how far the police should bend. One of the first limits involves language training. "If we decide to go to language training, then we have to determine how many people are to speak Russian, or German, or Spanish or Hindustani," says Stephen Hrehus. "Where do you draw the line? It would be easy to saturate this area with Russian-speaking officers. Great. Then what do you have? A little Russia. You have to reach a point where they have to come to you. You have to make them adjust to your situation."

Others feel strongly the other way. "The main issue to me is teaching cops to speak Spanish," says Lawrence Sherman, director of research for the Police Foundation in Washington, D.C. "There are just too many people out there who speak Spanish and who are involved in conflicts. Until we come to grips with that problem, how are we going to deal with smaller groups that speak different languages?"

Sherman's rhetorical question has economic as well as sociological implications. Although a few departments are busy adding programs oriented toward immigrant communities, most departments are hard-pressed to find the funds for such activities. With the dismantling of LEAA, federal assistance is no longer available for officers who want to learn a second language. The New York Police Department recently dropped a federally funded Spanish course and stopped paying extra duty pay to officers who were studying another language. In Santa Ana, Bassett says that because of the property tax cuts due to California's Proposition 13, "We are running bare bones and we can't hire enough [public service officers and interpreters] to address the entire community."

Some chiefs have turned to private foundations for support. In Minneapolis, Bouza says he is seeking private money to secure an interpreter for that city's Hmong population "because the budget is in a crisis...and I have no contact with the Oriental community. " Across the Mississippi River, St. Paul's McCutcheon says that if his city cuts support for the department's 24-hour Hmong interpreters, he will turn to private foundations as well.

The availability of public funds is only half the problem; the lack of public enthusiasm for such efforts is another. "The mood of the country and the churches [who have resettled refugees] is changing," says Mel

Lehman. "A few years ago it was, 'Be the first church on your block to support a refugee,' " Now, says Lehman, there is a growing dissatisfaction with federal immigration policies fueled by "the old cry: 'They're taking our jobs.' "

Some chiefs are worried that this resentment may generate discord in the new immigrant communities: "If the competition for jobs becomes greater, we are going to see ethnic groups [banding together] and with all of them competing for the same jobs, it could mean violence," says McCutcheon. One such incident occurred in Denver, in 1981, when groups of Chicano youths smashed apartment windows and vandalized property in a refugee community to protest what they thought was special treatment the refugees were getting in housing and welfare. A 1981 Orange County Human Relations Commission report asserted that "without immediate action...community tensions [between refugees and other ethnic groups] will likely escalate into violent confrontations." Miami police report that blacks and even other Hispanics are beginning to prey on Mariel refugees, because they see the Mariels as the cause of the city's economic and social stress.

Those tense conditions are aggravated by the federal government's cutbacks in welfare and food stamps, staples for many new immigrant communities. In Seattle, Noreen Skagen reports that a "desperation mood" is developing among the refugees there; in Orange County, one social service worker called conditions in one Southeast Asian ghetto "a breeding ground for mental illness" because of the poverty and tight quarters there. In Bellevue, Gary Felt fears the worst if the strain of unemployment and dwindling resources becomes too much: "Our shoplifting of food is going to skyrocket, and our suicide rate is going to go up. There will be an increase in police problems."

Ironically, the new immigrant communities are in need of police attention precisely when energy is being directed away from them. "It's absolutely essential, " says Joseph McNamara, chief of the San Jose, California police. "On both a professional and ethical level, we have an obligation to educate and reach out and establish relationships with them. Failure to do so can be tragic in terms of human experience."

CHAPTER 2

CHINATOWN: NO LONGER A COZY ASSIGNMENT

ROB WILSON

"I JUST CAN'T talk about it right now," said the San Francisco plainclothesman. "It's just too ticklish." He leaned back in his chair, narrowed his eyes and set his jaw tight. "I hope to God, though, I really hope they solve it."

"I know it sounds like a cliché," said a lieutenant down the hall, "but we're making progress."

"There's nothing more I want to say," said San Francisco Police Chief Charles Gain. "I think we've already said we're making progress.... We'll let it go like that."

Behind this "wall of silence," the San Francisco Police Department's investigation of the worst crime in the city's history crept along. It had been more than six months since three young masked Orientals casually walked into the Golden Dragon restaurant in Chinatown at a little before three in the morning of September fourth. They pulled out guns — one a shotgun — and fired crazily around the crowded room, bullets hitting the ceiling, walls and floor. When they left, eleven people were wounded and five were dead. Finally, after a major investigative effort, six suspects were arrested last spring.

The "Golden Dragon Massacre" is nobody's favorite subject in San Francisco. Just the mention of it causes Chinatown merchants and police to wince. That's not just because it was such a gruesome crime or that it left such an ugly stain on the city's number-one tourist attraction. It is because the murders struck at a very raw nerve — an eight-year pattern of Chinese youth gang violence which the police had not been able to crack.

21

The Golden Dragon incident raised the tally of Chinese gang-related murders in San Francisco to 37 since 1969. In an eight-year pattern of Chinese youth gang violence which the police had been unable to crack, only eight suspects have been convicted in those cases, and three of those convictions are now being challenged. At the time of the Golden Dragon shooting, police were blaming the investigative impasse on a "subculture of fear" in the Chinatown community.

Angered by the absence of witnesses or information, Chief Gain blasted the Chinatown community for "an absolute abdication of responsibility" last fall. "This is a tragedy we are constantly faced with," he told the press. "Chinese persons will not talk." That wasn't a new charge. As far back as 1974, the captain of the Chinatown police station house blamed the failure to stem the rising crime in the area on "failure of the people to be truthful, failure to report, failure to identify, failure to testify."

But this time, the issue blew up into a public relations fire storm. Gain, a liberal chief in only his second year in office, had stepped onto an old land mine with the Chinatown issue. Chinese-Americans exploded at what they considered "racial slurs." Said one Chinese spokesman: "We can hardly believe that the SFPD has retreated to century-old stereotypes in their public statements."

Throwing the responsibility back at the police, the spokesman said such statements "were self-serving and gave the impression that they were trying to excuse themselves from their duties as law enforcement officers."

Gain responded with a 21-member Gang Task Force to attack the gang problem. "We want to eradicate gangsterism in San Francisco," he said. "It may take years to do it."

The task force clearly was making some progress this spring. After an intense investigation, working with federal agents and informants, the task force tracked down the six suspects, all under 18, in March and April. Two were arrested in Reno, Nevada. Guns tied to the shooting were pulled from the mud off San Francisco Bay.

Despite the arrests, no one was pretending that the violence among Chinatown youths had ended. Shortly after the first Golden Dragon arrest, the thirty-eighth gang-related slaying took place on the steps of a San Francisco high school.

Chinese-Americans agree with Chief Gain that it will be difficult to "eradicate gangsterism" in San Francisco. But they tend to view the

problems differently. It will assuredly take years, they say, for the police
to bridge a gap created by a century of neglect and isolation of the
Chinatown community. And in that task, they are viewing police profes-
sions of "progress" with skepticism.

San Francisco police have come to accept at least some of the blame
for their bad relations with Chinatown. "We have the basic responsibility, " said Chief Gain. "I cannot indict or condemn the Chinese community. We are the ones that have to implement programs, convince people
of our sincerity, get results.... We have to achieve credibility."

The SFPD got a light push toward that goal in March when the Office of Civil Rights Compliance of the Federal Law Enforcement Assistance Administration compelled them to put some of their promises in
writing. To resolve a long-standing complaint from Chinatown leaders,
the LEAA and the SFPD signed a document in which the police agreed
to hire more Chinese-Americans, improve liaisons with Chinatown
groups and publicize available police services in both Chinese and English.

San Francisco is not the only city with the problem. Almost every
city with a sizable Chinese community has its own version. New York,
Los Angeles, Chicago, Toronto, Boston, Washington, D.C., Seattle,
Philadelphia, Atlanta have all reported Chinese youth gang activity.
New York police blame Chinese gangs there for more that 20 homicides,
at least 100 shootings and possibly hundreds of thousands of dollars taken in extortions and robberies in the past ten years.

Concern over the growing gang problem brought police together
from a dozen major cities to compare notes at a conference in Toronto
last fall. Another such gathering is scheduled for New York this September. Investigators from the FBI, the Federal Drug Enforcement Administration, and the Bureau of Alcohol, Tobacco and Firearms will
attend.

The explosion of youth violence in Chinatown in the past decade is
forcing the big-city police departments and the insular Chinese-
American community together for the first time. That has turned out to
be a tense confrontation, and a unique community relations and investigative chore. The three cities with the biggest Chinatown "colonies" —
San Francisco, New York and Los Angeles — have each approached the
task differently with varying success.

But in no city is the gang problem solved. And Chinatown leaders
fear that the gangs will continue to grow until the police have become a

part of the community. "I think if we let them go for a few more years," said Man Bun Lee, a prominent citizen in New York's Chinatown, "these gangs will be even worse than the so-called Mafia."

The gangs have exotic names, which seem to crop up and then fade away before the police get a chance to figure out who belongs to what. White Eagles, Black Eagles, Flying Dragons — such names might appear in several cities all at once, then disappear.

But three groups, or names, seem to have persisted. On the West Coast, in both San Francisco and Los Angeles, one gang has control inside the boundaries of Chinatown and another group operates outside, trying to get in. The leading group on the inside has been called Wah Ching, meaning "Chinese Youth," and is associated with the adult, fraternal tongs in Chinatown.

The outsiders have been called "Joe Boys," after a young Macao-born youth who was active in Chinatown several years ago and is now in prison.

In New York and throughout the East, the dominant gang is the Ghost Shadows. Wah Ching have also been known to operate in the East, and the Ghost Shadows have split into factions and are warring among themselves.

The numbers involved are hard to gauge. San Francisco police estimate there may be more than 300 kids in one gang or another there; Los Angeles figures it has about 150, New York about the same, and other cities, slightly less. In total there may be more than 1,500 Chinese youths involved in gang-related crimes across the country, although police say many of them are "associates" and not hard-core members.

The ages of known gang members range from 12 to 26. Police on both coasts believe that the youths have ties to adult groups involved in sophisticated crimes. They say some of the gangs are highly organized, mobile from state to state, and involved in extortion, robbery, narcotics and contract killing. Others are loose packs of young kids with no more apparent purpose than to shoot their rivals on sight.

How did the gangs form? Why are they fighting? Who are they? All are complicated questions that have different answers in different cities. But there are some common threads: Most of the gang members are recent immigrants from Hong Kong, and much of the early killing was attributed to hostilities between the "American born" and the "foreign born."

But it is also evident that the gangs did not emerge out of adolescent rivalries. The pattern of "insiders" in Chinatown fighting "outsiders" is strongly supported by the presence of adult criminal elements in Chinatown seeking to protect their turf. Police say the first gangs were started by adults to strengthen Chinatown rackets, and splits from those created the rival factions fighting today. Said one New York Chinese-American, "It was a case of the man training the tiger and the tiger eating the man."

Detective Neil Mauriello, part of a team especially assigned to the New York Chinatown gangs, equates them with Italian groups formed around the turn of the century. Like the Cosa Nostra in its formative stages, he said, the Chinese youths operate only against their own ethnic group; they have a quasi-military structure with a chain of command; they have strong interstate and international connections; they have been looking into legitimate investments for their criminal revenues; and they have enough money to make them "extremely mobile."

That mobility can be mind-boggling. Last year, suspects in extortions in Maryland and New Jersey were arrested in Chicago and New York. A murder by a gang leader in San Francisco was solved with a tip picked up in a Hawaii bar. The assailant of a prominent leader of New York's Chinese community was nabbed by border authorities in Washington state.

The international ties are less visible, but police and federal authorities know that gang leaders have crossed borders numerous times for questionable purposes. The youths are suspected of serving as heroin runners across the U.S.-Canadian border and leaders have made occasional trips to Hong Kong, allegedly to recruit new gang members for "social tasks" in the United States.

Authorities on both coasts suspect that youth gangs are being used in older, more established Chinatown crime operations, which are well-connected to the Orient. That, like most police matters relating to the gang issue, is a closely guarded secret. A two-month-old investigation by the New York City Public Morals Division into Chinatown crimes was "still highly confidential" in June, according to Lieutenant Martin Kennedy. "Events occurred which caused us to expand our investigation," Kennedy said. "This precludes us from terminating it in any way at all."

Exactly how much of a connection there is between the youth gangs, which consist for the most part of recent immigrants from Taiwan and Hong Kong, and older, more established Chinese organizations is a subject of constant speculation by police. Sometimes the youths are clearly operating in open defiance of the older criminal element, and sometimes they seem to be working under the direction of their older counterparts.

Much of the speculation about adult organized crime in Chinatown centers around the "tongs" — protective, fraternal orders that emerged in the last century. The tongs were considered a front for opium smuggling, gambling and achieved infamy for their territorial "tong wars" in the 1920s. Though the police cautiously emphasize the many above-board social activities of the tongs today, there is a strong feeling that the organizations are still involved in criminal activity.

In 1975, the Chief of a U.S. Justice Department Organized Crime Strike Force said, some of the facets of the tongs are more effective and efficient and sophisticated than the Mafia ever did think of being.

"Often," continued the federal official, Thomas Kotoske, "undercover investigation is impossible in Chinatown because the organization is just too tight."

Kotoske refused to elaborate recently on his earlier comments, which were made at a court trial. But after the Golden Dragon incident, Chief Gain said: "We have reasons to feel these kids are no more than pawns or cannon fodder.... It's not just a matter of juvenile delinquency. This is a complex thing that involves adults without question."

Although Gain also would not elaborate, an example of the sort of adult involvement he referred to might be a case back in 1971. After a group of Chinese youths started extorting money from businesses in the neighborhood of one of the San Francisco tongs, the tong took out an ad in one of the Chinese newspapers. It warned that if certain young people did not cease their illegal activities, they would be "severely dealt with." A few weeks after the ad appeared, three young Chinese men were found dead — hog-tied and dumped in San Francisco Bay.

That case, like numerous others, has not been solved. The theory on the streets is that the crime was committed by rival gang members, at the behest of the older "criminal element" in Chinatown. But police investigators could not prove it. Information and witnesses were not forthcoming, leads could not be confirmed, cases could not be developed.

That scenario has been repeated dozens of times on both coasts. The police found they could not penetrate the community where the crimes were occurring. But many Chinese-Americans say that because the police had so little understanding of the Chinatown community, they only resorted to oversimplifications, confusing the "criminal element" with the vast majority who are law-abiding citizens.

"It's very unfair of the police department, accusing the whole community of not cooperating," said Stephen Fong, president of the San Francisco Chinese Chamber of Commerce. Speaking through an interpreter, Fong said, "It's like asking an Italian community to point out the Mafia. You've got to be a part of the criminal element to recognize those people, and those are the last people who will come forward. Regular, law-abiding people don't know anything about these things."

But many Chinese-Americans will concede that there has been some reluctance to work with the police. Fear of retaliation, which affects any victim, is strong in Chinatown. Many people say they have reported crimes and the police failed to appear, or didn't follow-up. Chinatown residents who work long hours are also reluctant to sign witness reports, because they know that will mean appearances in court and days away from work.

Those are common problems police encounter in any community, and perhaps a bit more intensely in Chinatown. But there are other barriers that block the flow of information and evidence. The language problem is foremost. Between 40 and 50 percent of the residents in Chinatown don't speak any English, and Chinese-speaking police officers are almost nonexistent.

But the gap between the police and Chinatown runs deeper. More than just race or language there are cultural differences between East and West — ways of thinking, acting, living — that cause each side to view the other with suspicion and mistrust.

Probably more than any other ethnic minority, the 600,000 Chinese-Americans have clung to their cultural heritage. Ties to their homeland are strong. Some families have ancestors who immigrated from China in the last century, but most fled Communist China with Chiang Kai-Shek and went to Hong Kong or Taiwan. While the Chinese-American community is changing, old traditions and attitudes still survive in the Chinatown "colonies."

One of these attitudes, according to a merchant in San Francisco's Chinatown, was that "Chinese people don't like to work with officials — federal, state or local — at all. We had bad experience with them in China, so it's the same here." That particularly applies to the police. As one Chinese-American explained: "The police in Hong Kong never came to see you unless they were after you."

That is combined with the Eastern concept of "face," the notion of self-esteem and fierce pride which is the essence of Oriental character and which is little understood by Westerners. To be seen talking to the police could associate a Chinese person in the eyes of his neighbors with crime, and that would mean a loss of face.

The association of police with crime is also much different in Chinese eyes. Many Chinese-Americans remember the brutal tactics of the Hong Kong police, and say it was standard practice for the local police officer to take 10 percent of the vice proceeds on his beat.

That stereotype has persisted in Chinatown. Many residents, while they profess "respect" for the police, privately say it is common knowledge that police assigned to Chinatown have historically taken bribes to look the other way from gambling, narcotics, prostitution or sanitation and labor law violations.

"It's a protected enclave," said Harold Yee, a San Francisco economist who has made a study of Chinatown. "I'm sure you can perceive that some individuals have benefited from it.... For a long time, the Chinatown detail was one of the choicest assignments." The crux of the Chinatown graft issue is gambling. Different levels of gambling, from small, friendly Mah-Jong games to halls where professionals gamble for high stakes, have been a known activity in Chinatown for decades. Many residents say it is an accepted recreation in Chinese culture and should be left alone.

Charges of bribery are taken seriously by the police, who respond testily that what corruption there may have been has been eradicated. But, particularly after youth gangs became a problem, many residents of Chinatown have charged that the unmolested existence of the gambling is evidence of police involvement.

Police admit they have not given gambling a high priority. "Everyone knows it's there, so it survives," said New York's Mauriello. "Look, you've got Wall Street six blocks down. That's gambling. You've got Off-Track Betting (run by the state). That's gambling. You've got New Jersey putting in gambling across the river there. So, it's just not something we spend a lot of energy on."

But the gambling halls are known to be targets for extortion by the youth gangs. Because the operations are illegal, the victims don't report the extortion. To get at the gangs, the New York police have occasionally raided the halls "to impress upon the people that we're here," Mauriello said. "We tell them, 'Look, you're paying extortion to these gangs—tell us about it.' We let them know it would be better if they cooperate with us. It all comes down to one word: pressure."

In San Francisco, gambling was in the news after the Golden Dragon incident. Pressured by reporters, Mayor George Moscone said, "I know gambling exists. I've read about it in the newspapers. But if the police are winking at it, heads will roll."

The gambling in Chinatown is like the keystone to a very complicated structure. It is the point where crime, history, the police and the "community" converge. It is a symbol of a system that has existed for over a century and which is undergoing wrenching changes today.

That system goes back to the 1850s, when the first Chinese immigrants came to this country as unskilled labor to build the railroads. Discrimination from white laborers led to overtly racist laws. Until World War II, Chinese were denied citizenship, employment was restricted to menial labor, Chinese women were kept out of the country to control the population, and Chinese were officially barred from U.S. courts.

In that atmosphere, an inner Chinatown "establishment" emerged to provide the services denied by the outer society. "Family associations," credit unions, housing merchant groups, social clubs, and the tongs made Chinatown a self-contained world. Many of those groups were consolidated under one powerful paternalistic umbrella organization, "The Chinese Consolidated Benevolent Association" (CCBA), known in San Francisco as the "Chinese Six Companies." The organization had direct political ties to the Man-Chu Dynasty in China and later to the Nationalist government of Taiwan.

The CCBA came to wield immense power over Chinese-Americans. It controlled millions of their dollars, much of their property, housing, jobs, schools, hospitals, political and social life. Because Chinese were officially outside the purview of American justice, the CCBA also to a large degree represented the law inside Chinatown. With the exception of the bloody tong wars, violent crime was virtually unknown. Where there were disputes between community members, they were handled by the councils of the CCBA leadership. The elders rulings were final. The ultimate punishment was ostracism and the humiliating loss of face that went with it.

But there was crime in Chinatown, and in the early years it was almost synonymous with the tongs. Smuggling of opium and young girls (who were sold into prostitution) and the gambling operations were frequent activities of the "fraternal orders," police say. Scores of Chinese died when rival tongs fought with hatchets and guns in the 1920s. The violence and the vice subsided with time, but the aura remains.

The Chinese elders condoned the gambling and other crimes in Chinatown. Many Chinatown residents believed that some of those leaders themselves were (and are) deeply involved in the crime.

While the Chinatown establishment may have sustained the lives of the immigrants who poured into America, many residents today feel it was also exploiting them. The decisions of the elders let some prosper and forced others into disgrace. They acquired many enemies and stirred a growing resentment among the people they ruled, whose fear of the tongs or the powerful elders kept them silent.

Perhaps by default, the authority of the Chinatown elders was recognized by local governments and police. To many Chinese-Americans, the attitude that "the Chinese take care of their own" was a form of negligence which allowed crime to develop. "It's just a total concept of neglect," said Harold Yee, the San Francisco economist. "The lack of enforcement of the law, be it sanitary, wages or gambling, allowed the problem to flourish."

One of the main reasons people will not talk to the police, Yee said, is that the police are seen as part of the problem, not as part of the solution. "Either they are not prepared to deal with it, or in the eyes of many Chinese, they are a part of it," he said. "So how could you possibly go to the police and complain?"

The ability of the Chinatown establishment to "take care of its own" began to disintegrate after World War II. As discriminatory barriers to the surrounding society were lowered, successful Chinese-Americans started to leave the paternalistic grip of Chinatown.

As the tight community began to split up, U.S. immigration quotas were changed to allow more Asians to enter the country. Thousands of new immigrants — most with little money — began pouring into Chinatown in the mid-1960s, overwhelming the old internal structure.

Some people saw the youth gangs, in their early years at least, as symbolic of the ferment in Chinatown — a proud defense of "face" against all the prejudice and neglect their race had suffered, and a challenge to the outmoded authority of the Chinatown elders.

But nobody predicted the vicious independence that rebellion would assume. In the late sixties, the Chinatown establishment tried to coopt the youths. The tongs took them into their fold, forming young people's societies to keep them off the streets and bolster their flagging membership.

The youths, according to police, were employed in the gambling operations, where they were used as "look-see" guards and escorts for the winners. But it wasn't long before the gangs saw that they could make more money by robbing the winners and extorting payoffs from the gambling halls.

"At first, it was only fist fights. No guns, no shooting," said Man Bun Lee, for years the head of New York's Chinese Consolidated Benevolent Association. Through the early seventies, Lee said, "the elders wanted to recruit them, control them. But these kids are too damn smart."

The extortions and robberies soon spread out into businesses and restaurants. Rivalries over turf—who would have the rights to the most lucrative blocks in Chinatown—split one gang from another. Friction between the American-born and foreign-born Chinese smoldered into hatred, taunts, fights. Then, the gangs got guns.

The first gang murders happened in the early seventies in San Francisco and New York. On both coasts, they started in motion a pendulum of reprisals—shootings between one gang and another, some cold-blooded, calculated assassinations, some after seemingly chance encounters. It often didn't seem to make much difference who the victim was as long as he was one of the "enemy."

It soon became clear, at least to the Chinatown community, that the gangs were something they couldn't handle alone. In New York, M.B. Lee was the first "establishment" leader to recognize that. He sponsored several meetings to try and bring the police and the community together to fight the gangs.

Last summer, shortly after one of those meetings, a young Chinese man came to visit Lee in his Chinatown restaurant. In the respectful tones of the old days, he said, "Uncle man, may I speak with you for a moment?" Lee followed the youth into a hallway, where the young man pulled out an eight-inch knife and plunged it three times into Lee's stomach.

Lee recovered from the attack. Police caught his assailant several months later on the Washington-Canadian border. An illegal alien from Hong Kong who spoke no English, he pleaded guilty and was sentenced to four years in prison.

Lee does not believe that his attacker was just an angry youth. "There is something organized here," he said, "and the gangs are part of it. For one hundred years, the Chinese people have always taken care of their own business. Whenever we have had any disputes, we always settled it ourselves. I think that is what gave the American people the impression that we can take care of ourselves."

Then he looked across the room and said quietly, "Not any more. Not any more."

CHAPTER 3

THE VIETNAMESE CRIME NETWORK

GREG GROSS

YOU FLED your country as it fell to a Communist enemy and brought your family to the United States. You managed to start your own business, catering to your countrymen who settled in the same place. And business is good.

Then one day, the telephone rings. The caller speaks your native language. First, he praises your business, then he tells you how badly he needs money and how much of it he wants from you. Perhaps $300 a week, perhaps $500, perhaps more. Business is not THAT good; angrily, you refuse.

The caller then asks if you've heard about the store that was firebombed last month. Your business is good today, he says. Perhaps it will not be so good tomorrow.

Within days, a stranger will arrive at your door to pick-up the $300, or the $500, or more. He too will speak your language, probably a young teenager, fortified by liquor and the knowledge that police can do little to him because of his juvenile status.

Do you pay, knowing this is but the first installment on an extortionist's "protection" plan?

Do you stand your ground and refuse, knowing that eventually — maybe tomorrow, maybe next year — someone may put a gun to your head or hurl a flaming bottle of gasoline through your window?

Or do you turn to the police, whose language is still strange to you, whose methods are a mystery to you, and whose very appearance reminds you of the corrupt, brutal civil authorities whom you dreaded and avoided back home?

If you are Vietnamese, these are the choices you face the moment you become a target of the "Saigon cowboys," the low-key, sophisticated criminals who make their living by preying almost exclusively on their countrymen. They specialize in robbery, extortion, gambling, prostitution and occasionally murder. Their main weapons are veiled threats, bribery and the frightened silence of their victims.

If you are a police officer, you face your own problems with these gangs-victims whose language you cannot comprehend, a community of witnesses who see everything and say nothing, suspects who can be in Houston today, Los Angeles tomorrow and Portland the day after that, sheltered by relatives and friends, possibly using a different name in each place.

The problem is most acute in cities with established Vietnamese communities where the refugees have formed their own thriving business sector. "The vast majority of robberies and residential burglaries involving Vietnamese victims would have to be attributed to some kind of Vietnamese organization," said Detective Ferrell Buckels, a police investigator in the southern California city of Santa Ana.

It was Buckels who last year unraveled the kidnapping of an 11-year-old girl, Nguyen Anh Dao Thi. Her abductors had snatched her off the street on the way to school, demanding 200 ounces of gold for her safe return. Officers rescued the child from a house in nearby Anaheim. Three men and a woman were caught and convicted in the case. One suspect remains at large. "Some of these groups seem much better organized than others," Buckels said. "We know we're going to have problems. It's just a matter of time."

And law enforcement has made inroads against the gangs as Vietnamese businessmen slowly learn to trust police. A key success was the arrest last year of Tai Huu Nguyen, described by state organized crime analysis as "a major player in the gang leaderships," for the alleged attempted murder of a Vietnamese newspaper editor who spoke out against the gangs. But no one seems ready to declare the power of the gang broken.

"A year ago, they were shooting each other up in restaurants. That's not happening anymore, but it's hard to tell what's going on," says Tony Crittenden, an organized crime analyst with the California Justice Department. "Have we curtailed their activities or have they gotten wiser to what we're doing and gone more underground? We don't know."

There are signs, however, that the cowboys are expanding their activities, adding auto insurance fraud to their usual repertoire of robbery and extortion. And long-standing Chinese gangs in California have been recruiting Vietnamese members. "It's not fair to call it organized crime or a 'Vietnamese mafia,' " says Jack Shockley, police chief in the Orange County community of Westminster. "My gut feeling is yes, it exists, but I can't point to anything precise."

A bedroom community of about 72,000 people and very few Asians, Westminster experienced an almost overnight influx of Vietnamese in 1975 during the first refugee exodus from Vietnam. Today, the city is roughly 15 percent Vietnamese. Along Blosa Avenue, once-failing shopping malls are now filled with Vietnamese supermarkets, restaurants, offices and shops. On weekends, 30,000 to 50,000 Vietnamese from throughout the West pour into Westminster for "market days," buying goods they can find nowhere else.

The story is much the same in Orange County communities like Santa Ana and Garden Grove. In Los Angeles, Vietnamese businesses have supplanted the Chinese in virtually half that city's long-established Chinatown. For the refugees, the overwhelming majority of whom are proud and decent people, it's a success story. But their success also created a fertile hunting ground for the cowboys.

"In the late 1970s, we started picking up rumors, strong rumors," said Westminster Captain Donald Saviers. "The bakery owner would tell us about the tailor being shaken down. The tailor would say, 'No, not me. But the fabric shop down the street is.' "

Approaching the mid-1980s, Southern California cops have a rough idea of what they're up against. Says Shockley: "There's probably more prostitution there than is really visible. Gambling goes back 4,000 years in Asian cultures. And shakedowns have been a way of life in Vietnam since 1944. What we call a shakedown to them was just a way of doing business."

One group felt cocky enough this summer to try a little "business" against Che Linh, a major Vietnamese singing star. They threatened to bomb his performance at the Hollywood Palladium unless he paid $3,000. But Che Linh, known as "the Vietnamese Elvis Presley," stunned the hoods, his fans and authorities. He went to the police. The night of his concert, only 300 of the expected 3,000 people showed up, some expecting to witness Che's death. But there was no bomb; investigators nabbed two Vietnamese suspects who allegedly picked up the extortion payment. Before Che sang, he urged his fans to "stand up to the gangs." "There are only a few people in the gangs," he said. "But they shame all of us."

They also terrify most Vietnamese, who seldom volunteer information. Investigators often have to "wire" victims with hidden microphones and "tap" extortion calls to take a shakedown suspect to trial.

It's a frustrating situation for prosecutors like Bob Jones, a deputy district attorney in California's Orange County who specializes in Vietnamese gang cases. "We know extortion is going on, probably on a large scale. The number of gang members is fairly small, and everybody in the Vietnamese community knows who they are," he said. "But nobody wants to be a witness. Too often, you go into court and you haven't got anybody but a victim. It's not enough."

Unlike black or Hispanic street gangs, the Vietnamese don't advertise their presence with graffiti or garish dress. They don't adopt flashy nicknames for themselves and may not even give a name to their group. Nor do they devote much energy into defending gang territories.

They move at will through the Sunbelt states and the West Coast, creating an informal "circuit" from New Orleans and Houston to Southern California, north to San Jose and Portland, Oregon, west to Honolulu.

Wherever they go, the Vietnamese tradition of large "extended" families guarantees them ready lodging and sometimes a base of operations. "If they're of Buddhist background, they almost always seem to have a brother, a sister or a cousin somewhere," Saviers says. "They've got family scattered all over the country."

As they travel from place to place, they may align themselves with major figures in the Vietnamese community, doing whatever "job" he wants done. It might be a robbery, since the Vietnamese traditionally keep and trade in substantial amounts of gold. Or it might be a shakedown of a local merchant.

According to Jones, they also do a good job of keeping secret the identities of their leaders. "If you're a gang member, you only know who your immediate superior is," he said. "He calls you up and tells you to do things. And you do them, mostly out of fear. But you don't know who HIS boss is."

"These guys aren't like the Black Guerrilla Family or the Mexican Mafia, organizations with a structure and a hierarchy you can map out on a chart," said one of Shockley's investigators, a sergeant who asked not to be named. "You can't chart the Vietnamese."

Often, they identify themselves to their victims merely as working for a certain locally prominent Vietnamese figure. Depending on the clout of the individual whose name is evoked, that alone may be enough to instill fear and force compliance. If name-dropping doesn't work, the threats begin — and so does a major complication for law enforcement. Because when the gang members make their "propositions," the threats are often so indirect that proving extortion becomes a tough proposition in court.

In one case, a Westminster beauty shop owner came forward and named the men who were extorting her. They had shown her the butt of a gun tucked into a waistband and promised "to take care of her" if she didn't pay. That was enough for the police but not for the D.A.'s office, which refused to prosecute.

"For example, the word 'dang' has several meanings, depending on when the person uses it, the context he uses it in or how he pronounces it," Jones explained. "It can mean a party, a group, a political group or a gang."

Shockley's sergeant in Westminster had a more chilling example. "Someone may call you up and say, 'It's a beautiful day today, but the weatherman said it might rain tomorrow. If it rains, it will water the flowers. You might be around to enjoy the flowers, or perhaps you will fertilize them.'"

"To the Vietnamese, that's an absolute death threat. But you have a helluva time trying to convince twelve jurors of them."

You do NOT have to convince the Vietnamese. Mr. Nguyen had his Orange County grocery store firebombed when be balked at paying protection money. Like Che Linh, he sought help from police and got it, but the threat remains. He agreed to speak on condition that his real name not be used.

"The gangsters are under age, but the leaders are adults," he said. "They tell them, 'Because you are under age, the police can't do anything to you.'"

"These young ones, they don't want to go to school. They want to drink, be strongmen. Sometimes, they drink too much and someone dares them to shoot you. So they do it, just to show they are not afraid."

"Afterward, they are sorry. But that does not help me."

In addition to having the courage, Mr. Nguyen had enough confidence in his English to call police. Many Vietnamese don't. Orange County prosecutors tell of a woman who went from one police agency to another, trying to report a shakedown, only to be turned away because no interpreter was available and desk officers couldn't understand her.

Many Vietnamese also are confused and intimidated by the American justice system, which bears little resemblance to the French-based system of law in Vietnam. "In Vietnam, if someone's arrested on a major crime, he's taken away," said the Westminster sergeant. "When you're talking to your victim, the hardest thing in the world to explain is, 'Yes, he will be out on bail. Yes, there will be months before the trial. Yes, the trial may last several weeks.' "

"When they see a guy busted for extortion or robbery and he's back on the street in a few hours, two things are assumed. Either he got out of it or he's got so much juice with the police, he's like a 'godfather.' "

Even when extortion victims do speak out, investigators can't expect to rush out and nail the suspects. As Shockley's investigator explained it, the cowboys operate in a different sense of time than do Americans.

"If the extortion threat comes in at noon, you want to go out and set up a stakeout by one o'clock, but you can't do that with these guys," he said. "These people are prepared to wait you out for months, years. They have tremendous memories and they hold extortion threats like outstanding markers."

They also can pull up stakes and disappear on short notice until "the heat dies down." One of their favored cooling-off spots is Portland, Oregon, where police have confiscated weapons and arrested individuals wanted for felonies elsewhere. Another increasingly popular sanctuary is Mexico. Vietnamese suspected felons are known to frequent the bars in the Zona Norte, the seamy "red light" district of the border city of Tijuana.

But in pursuing the Saigon cowboys, borders present less of a barrier to police than language. Few police departments in the country have officers fluent in the varied dialect of Vietnamese. Most are forced to rely on a handful of private interpreters who may or may not be available when needed.

Some police departments, like that in Westminster, have been able to reach out to the Vietnamese community and develop a cadre of informants. It's a delicate relationship that calls for special care, according to Shockley's investigator.

"There's a bonding that takes place between you. The commitment is total," the sergeant said. "They're not only helping you on a case, but they're going against their own culture, everything they were taught. In their minds, they are committing a kind of treason. They will literally die for you."

Several departments are trying to convince Vietnamese residents to come forward when they have been victimized, and slowly, this is beginning to happen. The sight of well-known criminals being busted, convicted and put away helps.

But while close ties with the Vietnamese community are needed, Shockley warns against getting too close.

"We can be used as pawns through association," he said. "The money people in the Vietnamese community are very adept at using public association with public officials to their own advantage."

Westminster officials found this out the hard way after opening a regular series of meetings with local Vietnamese businessmen. "For a time," said one high-ranking officer, "we were eating egg rolls three times a week."

"Then we started getting back-door information that if we were seen with certain businessmen, that was taken to mean we were very 'friendly' with that individual. We've had to draw back considerably."

There is another danger to law enforcement. Gang members are not above trying to bribe American officials. One Southern California fire official was twice offered payoffs this year, once to ignore fire safety regulations at a restaurant and again to make a police case "go away." The fire officer reported the bribe attempt at once, undercover payments were set up and the suspects arrested. The case will soon go to trial.

"We've had investigators approached with plans that would make them very wealthy in a year's time," the Westminster sergeant said. "Police in America are paid a lot better than police in Vietnam, so we're really not as prone to that. But the possibility of corruption is definitely out there. There are big bucks involved. You've got to watch for it."

In summary, handling the Saigon cowboys requires special insights, techniques and sensitivity. But officers generally agree that the key to the problem is in the hands of the Vietnamese community itself.

"We hate seeing people victimized on a regular basis, but we're not in the victim solicitation business," Shockley said. "If people want to be protected, they're going to have to understand that they're no longer in Vietnam, and learn to play the game by American rules."

Section II
CASE STUDIES

CHAPTER 4

CHINATOWN'S IMMIGRANT GANGS: THE NEW YOUNG WARRIOR CLASS

DELBERT JOE AND NORMAN ROBINSON

OVER THE past decade and a half, Chinatowns in the major urban centers of North America have ceased to be islands of law and order and have instead become places in which crime is increasingly prevalent. The rise in crime is largely the work of gangs of immigrant Chinese youth who view themselves as a new young warrior class. The trouble began in the mid-1960s when both Canada and the United States adopted less restrictive immigration laws, under which substantial numbers of poorly educated and disaffected Hong Kong youth began to enter Canada and the United States (Rice, 1977:61). A number of these youths formed gangs which have created a wave of crime and fear in Chinatowns of San Francisco, Vancouver, New York, Los Angeles, and other cities.

PURPOSES OF THE STUDY

This study investigated the characteristics and process of four Chinese youth gangs (Phantom Riders, Golden Skippers, Blue Angels, Golden Wheels) in the Chinatown region of Vancouver (B.C.) over a four-year period (1975-1979). Specifically, the study attempted to answer three main questions:

1. What group characteristics do these Chinese youth gangs possess?

2. What is the nature of the group processes operating in these gangs?
3. To what extent can the sociocultural antecedents, functions, and characteristics of these Chinese youth gangs be explained in terms of current sociological theories of gang delinquency?

RESEARCH PROCEDURES

Data from five sources were collected and analyzed: (1) structured, in-depth interviews with a sample of members from each gang (a total of 13 members were interviewed by one of the researchers who speaks Cantonese); (2) structured interviews with individuals in the community who had contacts with the gangs (e.g. school personnel, youth workers, police); (3) school, police, and welfare records; (4) interviews with victims; and (5) on-site observation of gang activities.

FINDINGS

Group Characteristics of the Gangs

Member Characteristics. The members in all four gangs were immigrants recently arrived from Hong Kong. All were males between the ages of 13 and 19. There were no Canadian-born Chinese in the gangs, nor were there any gang members who had come to Canada during their preteen years. Moreover, the gangs did not contain any youths who had attended English schools in Hong Kong.

All of the gang members interviewed reported past or present school problems, particularly with learning English. About half of the gang members were dropouts. Those who were still in school attended irregularly. Gang members revealed that most of them were having problems with their parents. They said that their parents objected to their style of dress, their preference for Western food, their poor school performance, and their use of leisure time. They also reported problems in developing contacts with people their own age group. As immigrants, they attended special English classes, which lead them to be perceived by other students as members of an "outgroup."

Structural and Dynamic Characteristics. In terms of size, all four of the gangs had active core memberships of between 10 and 20 persons, with a larger fringe membership that participated in gang activities from time to time. Membership stability was relatively low, with a 25 percent turnover each year.

In terms of group uniformity, the gang members held very similar beliefs and attitudes. They felt discriminated against by the Canadian-born Chinese, the older China-born, and the larger Canadian society. On the other hand, the gang members expressed a strong desire to acquire stylish clothes, fancy cars, and other material symbols of success. They believed this could happen only if they learned English, obtained an education, and got a good job, but they felt blocked in this objective. Those gang members who were in school felt they were failures and objects of ridicule, and those who worked felt stuck in their menial jobs. As a consequence, the gang members felt they had to stand together for mutual support.

Behavioral Characteristics. School personnel reported a high incidence of "ah fai," a form of antisocial behavior practiced in schools. Imported from Hong Kong, "ah fai" behavior derives from movies (such as *The Blackboard Jungle*) to which Eastern influences (e.g. the martial arts, Oriental actors such as Bruce Lee) have been added.

With the Chinatown community, the four gangs were involved in extortion, shoplifting, picking pockets, possession of illegal weapons, refusing to pay for goods and services, beating of Canadian-born Chinese, trafficking in soft drugs, and gang fighting. The Phantom Riders were the only youth gang that had any contact with the young-adult gangs operating in Vancouver's Chinatown. Members of the riders would be recruited from time to time to assist a young-adult gang in its criminal activities.

During this study (1975-1979) the Blue Angels underwent considerable change. When first formed in 1971, the gang was very active in crime. In 1976, the gang came under the influence of a youth worker who involved them in a community program for the elderly in Chinatown. Soon after this, gang membership began to drop.

Group Processes in the Gangs

Interstimulation. In terms of the basic form of face-to-face behavior in the gangs, the observational data showed a good deal of playing at the martial arts. This activity was important, not only for fighting purposes, but also to develop and strengthen the gang members' image of themselves as "young warriors."

Recruitment. Each of the four gangs emerged from some community-organized activity for immigrant youth. The Phantom Riders and the Golden Skippers emerged from school classes. The Blue Angels began at the local YMCA. The Golden Wheels began at a local church. A fresh supply of recruits for the gangs came from new immigrants who came to the organized gangs.

Goal-setting. The data showed that the primary goals the gangs pursued were: (1) the acquisition of money and (2) manly image building. Money was needed for flashy clothes, cars, and so forth. The constant display of tough behavior was designed to show others that gang members were young warriors who commanded respect and fear.

Status Management. Contrary to the findings of some other gang studies (Thrasher, 1963; Cartwright, 1975), there appeared to be little strugggle for status within each gang. There were, however, distinct status differences between the gangs based on: (1) the degree of contact with young-adult gangs and (2) fighting ability. The Phantom Riders enjoyed the highest status. The Blue Angels also enjoyed high status, but it began to decline after 1976, when they became more involved in legitimate activities. The Golden Wheels increased in status from 1976 on as it established greater contact with young-adult gangs.

Analyzing the Gangs in Terms of Current Gang Theory

Sociocultural Antecedents. Most studies of delinquency among immigrant youth have stressed bad economic conditions, conflict of cultural norms, and conflict between parents and children as important factors contributing to the development of delinquency (Empey, 1978; Gibbens and Ahrenfeldt, 1966). Two decades ago, however, Eisenstadt (1959) suggested that immigrant delinquency among youth can be better understood in terms of :

(1) the diminution of the immigrant family's ability to satisfy the needs and aspirations of its members, particularly adolescents.

(2) the limitations of the social sphere and functions of the family, leading to the emergence of specific youth groups.

(3) the extent to which the immigrant group establishes a positive identification with the new society and the extent to which this identification is not blocked by the "absorbing" environment.

This study's data suggest that Eisenstadt's three points on the sociocultural antecedents of delinquency among immigrant children are particularly useful in explaining the origin and development of Chinese youth gangs. First, there is evidence that families in this recent wave of Chinese immigrants are not satisfying the needs of their members, particularly the adolescents. Fathers and mothers of gang members were found to be working long hours, often at two or three jobs each. Youngsters were left on their own and there was little supervision or guidance (Tisshaw, 1976:3). The traditionally close Chinese family unit did not exist.

Second, there was evidence to suggest a limitation in the traditional sphere and functions of the Chinese family. Social workers reported that the traditional Chinese extended kinship group did not exist among the families of the gang members. Rice (1977) and Sung (1976) have pointed out that recent immigrants from the pseudo-Western urban society of Hong Kong are dramatically different from pre-World War II immigrants, who came from the stable rural environments of China with their strong kinship ties. In this study, workers reported constant challenge of parental authority by gang members (Tisshaw, 1976). In earlier times, this rebellious behavior would have been dealt with by parents and relatives (Sung, 1967; DeVos and Abbot, 1966) or by self-appointed community courts (Sutherland and Cressey, 1955). The absence of kinship groups thus encourages the formation of adolescent peer groups which fill the social vacuum between the nuclear family and the community. But why do some peer groups become delinquent and others not?

A likely answer to this question emerges from an examination of Eisenstad's third point: the immigrant's degree of positive identification with the host society and the extent to which this identification is blocked by the "absorbing" society. The Chinese people see education as the key to success, and parents will make almost any sacrifice to ensure that their children receive schooling. The parents of the gang members studied here expected their children to succeed in school. The difficulties the youth encountered in learning English made success unlikely. They saw around them the material and status evidence of what success in school could bring, particularly among Canadian-born Chinese, but success was denied them because of their inadequacy in English. As Cloward and Ohlin (1960) point out, delinquent groups develop when a society establishes success goals for youth and at the same time provide youth with few legitimate opportunities to attain them. In the absence of legitimate opportunities for attaining the success goals, delinquency becomes an alternative means of attaining them.

Gang Characteristics. The data from this study tend to support the concept of the gang as a near group (Haskell and Yablonsky, 1974). The gangs had shifting memberships, distributed leadership, diffused expectations and roles for members, limited group cohesion, and a variable life span. Like the gangs studied by Miller (1975, 1977), the Chinese youth gangs were less concerned with "turf" than with money. As such, the gangs could be typologized as essentially criminally oriented (Cloward and Ohlin, 1960). Like the criminal gangs of Spergel (1964), the Chinese gangs had two principal suborientations: (1) racketeer and (2) theft. The Phantom Riders had contacts with the young-adult gangs and thus ample opportunity to learn and use the illegitimate means (racketeering) needed to achieve success goals (money, manly status). The other three gangs had no contacts with adult gangs, and therefore, theft became their way of attempting to achieve success goals.

CONCLUSION

By late 1979, none of the four gangs existed as it had in 1975. The Blue Angels had dispersed and members largely entered the work force. The Golden Skippers still existed but were not active. Many in both the Phantom Riders and the Golden Wheels had graduated to young-adult gangs.

The problem of Chinese youth gang formation is likely to continue if Canadian and American immigration policies remain as they are. Youth will be admitted who have only a limited chance to succeed in the host country.

Gang information can be inhibited only if immigrant youth are able to

find and acquire new, permanent and recognized social roles and to participate in close personal relations with the old inhabitants. The existence of personal channels through which the immigrants can be introduced to new social settings is the prerequisite of absorption. In many cases, the existence of such channels mitigates the results of unfavorable family settings...and the negative identification between the families and the commumity. (Eisenstadt, 1959)

REFERENCES

Cartwright, D.S. "The Nature of Gangs," in D.S. Cartwright et al. (Eds.): *Gang Delinquency*. Belmont, CA: Wadsworth, 1975, pp. 1-22.

Cloward, R.A., and Ohlin, L.E. *Delinquency and Opportunity*. New York: Macmillan, 1960.

DeVos, G., and Abbott, K. "The Chinese Family in San Francisco." M.A. thesis, University of California, 1966.

Eisenstadt, S.N. "Delinquent Group Formation Among Immigrant Youth, in S. Glueck (Ed.): *The Problem of Delinquency*. Boston: Houghton Mifflin, 1959, pp. 200-209.

Empey, L.T. *American Delinquency: Its Meaning and Construction*. Homewood, IL: Irwin, 1978.

Gibbins, T.C., and Ahrenfelft, R.H. *Cultural Factors in Delinquency*. London: Tavistock, 1966.

Haskell, M.R., and Yablonsky, L. *Crime and Delinquency*. Skokie, IL: Rand McNally, 1974.

Miller, W.B. "The Rumble This Time." *Psychology Today*, *10*(March): 52-59s, 1975. In *Violence by Youth Gangs as a Crime Problem in Major American Cities*. Washington, D.C.: U.S. Government Printing Office, 1977.

Rice, B. The new gangs of Chinatown. *Psychology Today*, *10*(March): 60-69, 1977.

Spergel, I. *Racketville, Slumtown, and Haulburg*. Chicago: University of Chicago Press, 1964.

Sung, B.L. *Mountain of Gold: The Story of the Chinese in America*. New York: Macmillan, 1967, p. 179.

Sutherland, E.H., and Cressey, D.R. *Principles of Criminology*. New York: Random House, 1955, pp. 74-81.

Thrasher, F.M. *The Gang*. Chicago: University of Chicago Press, 1963, p. 230.

Tisshaw, K. "Recently Immigrated Chinese Youth and Strathcona experience: A Report to the Strathcona Youth Services Advisory Committee," (mimeo.), 1976, p. 3.

CHAPTER 5

ISOLATION AND STIGMATIZATION IN THE DEVELOPMENT OF AN UNDERCLASS: THE CASE OF CHICANO GANGS IN EAST LOS ANGELES*

JOAN W. MOORE

I BECAME interested in the relevance of the labeling perspective after looking again at John Kitsuse's 1979 SSSP presidential address. He was surprised and a little delighted when he noticed that stigmatized persons were collectively rejecting the labels that he and other theorists of deviance had analyzed so effectively. "Deviants were coming out all over...to profess and advocate the lives they lived and the values that those lives express" (Kitsuse, 1980).

One of the controversial issues in his paper and to other labeling theorists was the extension of the labeling analysis to minority persons. They implied that to be a minority person—or a woman, for that matter—is to be stigmatized. Thus, Goffman talks about "tribal stigma of race, nation and religion" (1963), and Kitsuse adds "genetic stigma" to include gender, left-handedness, and other genetically determined attributes (1980). This is a rather blurry area, particularly in the case of minorities. Labeling and its consequences for generating distinctive lifestyles (or secondary deviance) evoke images of deviance, not "otherness."

*This chapter is a revision of the presidential address to the Society for the Study of Social Problems, Washington, D.C., August, 1985. I have profited greatly from the comments of the following people, none of whom is responsible for the remaining flaws: Robert Garcia, Ron Glick, Ralph Guzman, John Kitsuse, Ellie Miller, Greg Squires, Paul Steele, Marc Thomas, Diego Vigil, and Doris Wilkinson. Correspondence to: Department of Sociology, The University of Wisconsin-Milwaukee, P.O. Box 413, Milwaukee, WI 53201.

As Kitsuse acknowledged, many people were uneasy about this extension. After all, women and minorities were not really deviants. And are the subcultures of minorities "secondary deviance"? Some interpretations of the labeling perspective imply that these subcultures would not have emerged without public labeling. Obviously, this is not true.[1]

However, there may be some truth in this perspective that is worth untangling. Stigma involves a stereotype, and for minorities the stereotypes include perceptions of deviance. The larger society certainly does label some minority persons, a priori, as "probably deviant." Thus to be young, male, and black or Chicano in white America is to be a suspect person (cf. Wilkinson, 1977). To be a visible member of a population that many Anglos associate with violent crime is to evoke hostile and fearful responses. I would like to call this "ascribed deviance" and to distinguish it from the "achieved deviance" of the criminal or the drug addict.[2] The ascription of deviance is based, of course, on generalized stereotypes, but it is focused on a particular segment of the minority population. Ascribed deviance, then, is deviance that is ascribed to minority young men on the basis of visible characteristics (or, if you like, ascriptive characteristics). Young black males need only appear in an Anglo neighborhood to evoke fear.

The ascription of deviance to young minority males by Anglos has some direct consequences. We might reasonably expect that these consequences would be trivial for law-abiding minority youth, even if all Anglos thought that all minority young men were likely to be violent or criminal. Young men in the "wrong" place — e.g. wandering in an Anglo neighborhood — might be harassed. However, real damage is done when suspicious Anglos control the police, schools and organize services for youth, and structure these institutions in order to avert and control possible deviance. The functions of these socializing institutions are thus distorted and the result is socialization destined for social control.

There are also indirect effects, which operate through community social structure. How do the law-abiding members of minority communities react when their children are groundlessly assumed to be deviant? I suspect that they turn on the "real," achieved young deviants in their midst. After all, isn't it those "real" deviants and their deserved reputation that caused all this trouble with the Anglo community in the first place? The targeted ascription of deviance by Anglo — to young minority males — generates processes inside minority communities which are very different from the consequences of general discrimination. General discrimination makes minority people mad at Anglos, but ascriptive labeling makes those same minority people mad at other minority people. Achieved deviants and innocent members of their families become the target of enhanced labeling within the communities—labeling which might not have occurred without the Anglo ascription of deviance. This generates more secondary deviance, laying the conditions for the development of a distinctive underclass.

But minority communities are internally differentiated, and some people are highly likely to transmit and amplify the Anglo labeling, while others correctly view it as yet another form of racism. Three crosscutting bases of differentiation concern me. First, there is the distinction between respectable and disreputable poor found in writings on the American class structure from Warner (Warner and Lunt, 1941) through Matza (1966) and Banfield (1970). The distinction refers not only to law-abiding vs. law-violating behavior but even more importantly to variations in the degree of "concern with 'front' and respectability," as Drake and Cayton make clear about the black middle class (1962). I suggest that it is those who are preoccupied with maintaining their own front of respectability that are the most likely to transmit Anglo labeling.[3] Thus, the distinction between law-abiding people and law breakers is reinforced and given much more moral impact by the desire of some to prove to themselves, to each other, and to label-prone Anglo contacts that they, at least, are decent people.

The second crosscutting basis of differentiation is the equally familiar cut between accommodationists and the protest oriented. Many poor people (both white and minority) define the reward structure of the dominant system in "either deferential or aspirational terms" (Parkin, 1972), and adjust to inequality without interest in collective improvement. But many minority persons define the dominant system as unfair and are preoccupied with changing it for their group.[4] Many law-violating and law-abiding persons are accommodationist, while both law-violating and law-abiding persons have protested injustice and racism. Accommodationists are most prone to transmit the labels, while the protest oriented are more likely to become alienated from the larger system.

There is a third dimension of differentiation within poor minority communities. Many people in these communities are first-generation urbanites. During and after the Second World War large-scale migration of blacks and Hispanics to American cities filled the ghettos and barrios with newcomers. More recently, a heavy influx of non-European immigrants is having a similar impact on the composition of American cities in the 1980s (cf. Maldonado and Moore, 1985). Invariably, this means that newcomers—law-abiding and law-violating alike—struggle with both urban ways and American ways. Many also bring highly traditional and individualistic values.

I think that Kitsuse (1980) and others missed these distinctions. But this is understandable. Kitsuse, for example, focused on the processes during a peculiar point in history, the days of "the Movement"—the Great Egalitarian Movement of the 1960s and early 1970s. When he gave his presidential address to the SSSP in 1979, Kitsuse was very much impressed by the effects of the "politics of social and legal entitlement." Stigmatized deviants (gays and young blacks in Hunters Point, for example) were collectively "confront[ing]...asses[ing]...and reject-[ing]...the negative identity embedded in secondary deviation and were transform[ing]...that identity into a possible and viable self-conception." He called this "tertiary deviance" the flaunting of a stigmatized life-style and the transcendence of stigma.

Since much of Kitsuse's argument draws on the Egalitarian Movement, it may be worth looking at that epoch a little more closely and see who was flaunting what stigmatized life-style. Thus, among minorities, it is true that conventional demonstrators (conflict and political groups) marched side-by-side with groups of actual, achieved minority deviants.[5] But there is something very peculiar about the "tertiary deviance" that was expressed in these public affirmations of minority identity and solidarity. At least among the Chicanos, it was not achieved deviants such as ex-convicts and gang youth who flaunted the street style—they wore conventional clothing. It was the college students, symbolically associating with the stigmatized Chicano gang youth, who adopted the street style. Their style was a challenge to "colonialist" teachers and accommodationist relatives, a courting of ascription of deviance from Anglos that was designed to separate themselves from hints that they aspired to assimilationist life-styles.[6] By contrast, the style of the achieved deviants was not designed for an Anglo audience. Rather, they were coming out more cautiously to the respectable people living inside the minority community. For Kitsuse, tertiary deviance involves an affirmation of a stigmatized life-style. This is not too hard for college students, plainly on their way to respectability, but much harder for the achieved deviants — the street people and ex-offenders, blacks and Hispanic. There are two steps in the transformation of this stigmatized identity. First, respectable minority persons must be convinced that the street life-style does not necessarily involve danger to the community, and that these persons should, indeed, be reintegrated. Only then, with respectable allies, can gang youth and ex-offenders directly confront the labeling of the larger society. There had to be two steps, because the initial labeling of these achieved deviants went through two steps over many years. The first step involved continuous labeling by Anglos of all young minority males as probable deviants. The second step was continuous reactive labeling of gang people inside the minority community, further isolating and stigmatizing achieved deviants. Therefore, as a first step to redress, the street people of the 1960s made claims for acceptance in a specialized role in the Movement — as militants. The claims were successful: young college militants redefined the gang people as "specialist" in resistance to authority and symbolically adopted the street style.[7] This second step, then, meant that ex-offenders and gang members had found respectable minority allies to confront the larger system about their grievances. In turn, the ex-offenders backed up Chicano professionals and paraprofessionals in their confrontations with health care institutions, schools, and community development agencies.

Ultimately, the Movement provided an opportunity for minority communities to reabsorb their achieved deviants. However, this was not to last. Minority responses to both achieved and ascribed deviance are complicated and fluctuate from time to time. We must analyze the cross-cutting social differentiation within the communities in order to understand this. Under some conditions the community labelers prevail; under others, their influence is submerged. Similarly, there are variations in the extent to which minority-achieved deviants "come out" as they did in the days of the Movement, or remain mired in secondary deviance that begins to resemble an underclass subculture. To ground this discussion, I will turn to a more detailed history of the gangs in Chicano East Los Angeles.

CASE HISTORY: GANGS IN EAST LOS ANGELES

Youth gangs are particularly susceptible to labeling as deviant, regardless of their behavior. In Chicano communities of the 1980s, a "disreputable" life-style is closely associated with the development over the past two generations of a **cholo** or street life-style which derives from the youth gangs (Vigil, 1985a & b). **Cholismo** includes considerable pessimism about adult life changes, anticipates some time in prison, and incorporates deep fatalism about the prospects for conventional careers. The **cholo** life-style approaches but cannot yet be called the culture of an "underclass" or "lumpenproletariat" either on subjective or objective grounds. Youth gang members neither feel ostracized nor do they all in fact graduate to an adulthood of degradation. The following history may sound like a classic illustration of deviance, labeling, and secondary deviance. But the point of it is that the gangs evolved within a community that was extremely sensitive and responsive to Anglo ascription of deviance to its members.

I will trace four turning points in the evolution of these gangs.[8] All four are related both to changes in actual or achieved deviance and to the ascription of deviance from the larger society. The first two developments permitted the labelers within the community to stigmatize the gangs, the third reversed the trend and reintegrated gang members, and the fourth again isolated the gangs. Community differentiation figured into each turning point, as did the behavior of gang members. Newcomers, old-timers, accommodationists, and protesters all played distinct roles.

The "gang" in Mexican and Mexican American life is not necessarily delinquent. Aggressive male youth groups have been a documented feature of town and rural life as far back as the nineteenth century (Redfield, 1941). They appeared in rural Texas in the guise of **palomillas** (Rubel, 1965) and continued in American cities, attached to specific neighborhoods or barrios as they had been in Mexican cities. In Los Angeles in the 1920s Bogardus (1926) called them "boy gangs" to distinguish them from "real" gangs. In the 1930s the precursors of the three Los Angeles gangs we have studied were respectable groups of young men. In fact, in one of the neighborhoods, White Fence, the gang was attached to the barrio church and called by the church name, **La Purissima**, as late as the 1940s. The early barrio gangs of the Mexican agricultural laborers of Los Angeles's San Fernando Valley in the 1930s were much like the rural **palomillas**. We know they formed a baseball league, and outside the league they went from one town to another crashing Saturday night dances and fighting with each other (Moore et al., 1979a). Even the local police didn't seem to make much fuss about the gangs.[9]

Then, in the 1940s, the gangs developed a style that soon evoked a sharp reaction from the Anglo community. It is the first clear instance of ascriptive labeling. This was the **pachuco** fad. It swept the second-generation youth style throughout the community, although the gang youth may have been particularly fond of the exaggerated "drapes" and double-soled shoes.[10] But the gangs did not seem to be deviant. To be sure, there were fights, occasional serious wounds, and even deaths. But this was in the tradition of aggressive barrio-based youth groups. The **pachuco** gangs of the 1940s were sharing a version of the larger youth culture (zoot-suiters) that involved innovation in language and life-style. Not surprisingly, Mexican-born parents were often baffled (Burma, 1954: Griffith, 1948). The 1940s Chicano gangs were culturally innovative; however, our research suggests that the innovation remained strictly within a Mexican youth tradition. Thus, in the semi-rural San Fernando Valley, the **pachuco** Polviados of San Fernando were seen as "peculiar"—even a little sisified—by other San Fernando Valley gangs, because they "dressed fancy and smelled pretty" and spent a lot of money to achieve these effects. They were no longer Mexican gangs but Chicano gangs (Moore et al., 1979a). Still, no one inside or outside these gangs seems to have defined them as dangerous, even when a subclique began to use heroin. Heroin use, in fact, seems to have been an extension of older patterns of marijuana use. Casual use was overlooked.

Zoot-Suit Riots

This comparatively halcyon state was not to last. The sweep arrests accompanying the Sleepy Lagoon murder case and the later zoot-suit riots of the early 1940s were the first turning point in the Anglo labeling of young Mexicans as deviant (Acuna, 1981; Gonzalez, 1981; Mazon, 1976; McWilliams, 1949). Mexican communities east of downtown Los Angeles were invaded by servicemen. Youths wearing the zoot-suit costume anywhere in the city were chased and beaten, regardless of their behavior. Most of the victims were not members of gangs. Newspapers went well beyond the facts of the race riots and greatly stirred up racial feelings. For instance, the term "ratpack" was coined by a reporter to refer to Mexican youth gangs. The net result was a new and strongly established image of Mexican young men as savage. This ascription of deviance was never reversed. It was said to be genetic—"blood lust" inherited from the Aztecs. While there is no doubt the Chicano gangs were aggressive, this was the first time gangs and youthful Mexican violence became part of the media stereotype (Gonzalez, 1981).

How did this development affect the barrios? These were new labels and many Mexican Americans reacted with great concern. Thus, when the Anglo press labeled Mexican American youth gangs as "vicious," many respectable people accepted the label.[11] They may have felt it was exaggerated, but it was important that they dissociate themselves. Over the next decade, the increase in police harassment and sensationalist press coverage reinfored this reaction. As one young activist put it in 1954, "It is becoming more and more difficult to walk through the streets of Los Angeles—and look Mexican!" (Guzman, quoted in Acuna, 1984). Basically the respectables thought that the police harassment made no distinction between good kids and bad kids. Therefore, people who needed a respectable front may have been especially punitive toward the youth gangs.

But, on the other hand, many people in the barrios tolerated the gangs for years. They saw the gangs as little more than nuisances and defined the police reaction as racist.[12] Throughout this period gang members recall that perfectly respectable barrio residents **did** hide them from police and **did** lie in order to protect them (Moore et al., 1979b). Of course, in small communities, even outside the Mexican barrios, perfectly respectable people are likely to know somebody with a kid in the local gang or to have a child or relative in the gang themselves. At that time there were few if any "gang families" or families with a **cholo** tradition of street life over several generations. We must not forget that to be upwardly mobile in those days usually implied movement into the Anglo world, since opportunities within Chicano communities were limited. Thus, there was probably concern with "front" and correspondingly greater sensitivity to Anglo stereotypes. In addition, there was a continuing trickle of new immigrants from Mexico to cluck in disapproval at the youthful violators of tradition.

Heroin Indictments

During the 1950s still other processes were at work inside the gangs. Increasing stigmatization and isolation probably encouraged further deviance. Most importantly, the spread of heroin in the barrios generated intensified law enforcement (see Moore et al., 1979a). This lead to a second turning point in ascriptive labeling. Some major changes in police practice lead to widely publicized indictments of young gang men for heroin marketing in 1950. Other cases were also widely publicized. Subsequently, California narcotics laws became more punitive and, for the first time, barrio men went to prison in large numbers. Barrio gang subcultures began to incorporate mythologies about coping with prison. This had predictable effects on younger members. The earlier naivete of the gangs was destroyed; tension and secrecy mounted, and there was even greater reliance on "homeboy" networks. Mexican Americans long had been stereotyped as marijuana users, and now the image of the evil dope dealer was added to the "ratpack" image of the gangs.

Chicano Movement

The community reaction to these gangs was now negative. But, by the late 1960s the community reversed itself for a third stage. As noted earlier, street gangs and ex-offenders were integrated into the Chicano Movement. This happened for several reasons. First, gangs began to be romanticized as social bandits in the century-old Mexican tradition of resistance and opposition to Anglo authority.[13] This romanticization was partly a revisionist account of accommodationist histories of the barrio — an attempt to demonstrate an unbroken history of Chicano resistance to Anglo repression.

Second, gangs (and their ex-offender adult members, the **pintos**) had a specialized role: they were seen as a sort of fighting branch of the Chicano Movement. **Pintos** responded to the image of themselves as "soldiers." The Brown Berets (gang members and younger ex-offenders) marched and solemnly posted guards during rallies. In the bloody riot of August 29, 1970, a line of **pintos** spontaneously came out of the crowd to keep a police charge at bay, giving the women and the children in the crowd a few minutes to escape before being overrun. Only two weeks later an ex-offender organization undertook to organize security for a Mexican Independence Day parade, drawing on a network of Chicano gangs in the Los Angeles metropolitan area. This general eagerness to defend the entire community **(la raza)** was at least in part an extension of the gang's propensity to defend its own tiny neighborhood or turf.

The **pintos** and the young men of the barrios were integrated into the Chicano Movement through other means than a romantic ideology and their specialized role as soldiers. Kinship linkages also contributed to this end. Relatives of members of ex-offender self-help groups were scattered throughout the growing set of community-based organizations established as part of the war on poverty. In addition, some of the paraprofessionals in these new agencies had themselves been gang members as teenagers and were unusually sensitive to the needs of their clientele.[14] Many older, conventional Mexican Americans—some in professional positions—appeared in support of these groups. An ex-offender organization held a weekly **menudo** breakfast, served by women relatives. For many relatives of the ex-offenders, this was the first chance to come out into the open about the incarceration of a family member. The family shame could be redefined as a community issue. Many community leaders saw the Chicano Movement as an extension of their lifelong struggle for the advancement of Mexicans and sympathized with the **pintos** as a segment of the community needing reintegration into barrio life—not rejection or further stigmatization. These networks facilitated the reintegration of achieved deviants into a protest-oriented community movement.[15]

Very clearly, this appears to be what Kitsuse calls "coming out all over" or the development of "tertiary deviance." But was it? Ex-offender groups were actually being consciously political, trying to gain broad community support for prison reform, for change in laws about sentencing narcotics offenders, and for community programs for gang youth, ex-offenders and addicts. It was during this era—the early 1970s—that heroin addiction began to be recognized and defined as a serious problem within these communities, and local medical people began to deal with it as a medical issue rather than as a purely criminal activity. Thus, Kitsuse's tertiary deviants, the militant squares adopted the style of younger gang members in their symbolic "tertiary deviance" to mark their identification with the politics of entitlement. But older gang members worked with change-oriented squares to reintegrate **pinto** and addicts into conventional careers.

Prison "Super-Gangs"

However, this was not to last. During the last ten years or so, the push toward accepting the "achieved deviants" back into the community has waned. A wave of violence in California prisons heralded a fourth turning point in the history of barrio gangs. Community-based convict and addict organizations were swept away, as **all** ex-offenders were suspected of association with the prison-based Mexican Mafia or **La Familia**, two prison "super-gangs" (Adams, 1977). Once again, Anglo authorities and the media ascribed deviance to all Chicano convicts—overgeneralizing from the real, achieved deviance. Each of the five cultural and structural bases for the movement-inspired integration of the gangs into the community dissolved. First, the street people were again defined as criminals rather than as social bandits. Now this criminal definition was even stronger. When some younger researchers recently showed an interest in studying and working with ex-offenders, older Chicano scholars advised against it. They argued that **pintos** are just "limpenproletariat" — a liability and not a resource for the Chicano Movement.[16] Second, there were no more street demonstrations and the **pintos** lost their value as soldiers. Third, families of ex-offenders[17] reverted to an earlier adaptation: hiding their shame. Fourth, former gang members who had turned respectable and "come out of the closet" to support people were now discredited for their association with individuals later proven to be linked to the Mexican Mafia. Fifth, many of the older paraprofessional activists retired, and community-based organizations became increasingly professionalized. Federal and state funds were cut and paraprofessional street workers, who were generally more empathetic with the gangs, were forced into marginal positions or eliminated.

In sum, there was a major erosion in the presence and legitimacy of structural and cultural resources for integrating street people into conventional roles. The end result was predictable: prison self-help groups dissolved and community-based agencies serving ex-offenders were eliminated, only to emerge, transformed, as part of the criminal justice system. Gang programs began to be replaced by sheriff's and police department anti-gang efforts, which were strengthened in the 1980s. Gang isolation increased, as did gang violence.

Other shifts in community differentiation reinforced these trends. The increased pace of immigration from Mexico in the 1970s meant that the barrios began again to fill with men and women who were very traditional in their values and generally contemptuous of Americanized Chicanos — and of the **cholo** gang members in particular. No matter how poor they might be, Mexican immigrants often display an attitude of superiority toward Chicanos whom they view as inept with the Spanish language and unfamiliar with Mexican ways. Some community activists feel that this immigrant rejection of **"pocho"** or Chicano culture underlies the refusal of newer community groups to take up the cause of reintegrating street people. Thus, in Los Angeles the church-based UNO (United Neighborhood Organization, affiliated with Saul Alinsky's Industrial Areas Foundation) actively rejected work with gang youth and, in fact, asked for enhanced policing as a solution to the gang problem, even though UNO and its counterpart organizations have played a different role in other cities. These changes all occurred against a constant barrage of media coverage, which continues to sensationalize the barrio gangs and dramatize police response. Similarly, the media paint lurid pictures of prison gangs and applaud the "get tough" correctional responses.

In sum, we find four critical turning points in the reputation of gangs in Chicano East Los Angeles: the zoot-suit riots, the large scale indictments of gang men for heroin dealing, the political "coming out" and reintegration of gang members during the Chicano Movement, and finally, the appearance of the violent prison gangs and corresponding repression in the community. Three of these four turning points involved further isolation and intra-community stigmatization of the gangs. Across these four periods, media coverage of the gangs has always been negative.

This is a rather depressing history, but it does not imply that law-abiding Mexican Americans in East Los Angeles are eternally and unremittingly hostile to gang youth, any more than it shows overwhelming acceptance of gangs during the heyday of the Chicano Movement. There are always mixed feelings. Thus, when PCP recently became a major drug in East Los Angeles, there was a wave of sympathy for the youngster (and their families) who were caught up with this dangerous drug. The sympathy soon faded. Gangs, gang members, and their families are more and more isolated, and increasingly are left to the attention of law enforcement. Remnants of an integrative approach survive in a few programs that hire or work with young gang people, but these efforts run against the dominant trend. The East Los Angeles version of gang culture has spread into other communities in the metropolitan area, into other cities of the Southwest, and even into the border cities of Mexico. Thus, East Los Angeles is a center for the diffusion of the **cholo** subculture. Predictably, it is also a center of information and techniques for reactive institutions — specifically, the media, the police, and the prisons that wish to combat gang violence.

PROCESS AND MINORITY COMMUNITIES

It is often argued that we should not look at the processes within minority communities for the answers to their problems. Many researchers feel the answers obviously lie elsewhere. This argument is particularly persuasive in the late 1980s when we try to disentangle the twin effect of drastic shifts in the economy and changes in the political support structures. But this view implies that these communities are passive victims of external social conditions, and this is not entirely true. If an underclass is developing in poor minority communities, respectable members of these communities will react. Exactly how they react depends both on the cues from the larger society and on their own location within the community social structure. In the history just sketched, a major indirect effect of ascriptive labeling of minority youth has been to exacerbate cleavages within minority communities. In the 1940s diffuse racist sentiments became focused, with media and institutional targeting on the youth; what was "just another riot"—a seven-days' wonder—to the press had devasting impacts on the communities involved. In the scramble to establish that there were "good" Mexican kids and that "race" wasn't the issue, respectable Hispanics stigmatized and isolated the "bad" kids—the then comparatively innocuous gang kids and their almost totally innocent families. Then, during the 1960s and the politics of entitlement, the community was reminded that race is the stigma, and the achieved deviants and their families were reintegrated both symbolically and structurally. Once again, this alliance has disintegrated as have the policies and program that helped to promote it.

The case of East Los Angeles is not an isolated instance, only of esoteric concern. In city after city, the minority youth gang is either clearly defined as a social problem, as in Los Angeles and Chicago, or is currently being created, as in my own city of Milwaukee (Office of Juvenile Justice and Delinquency Prevention, 1983). In these "new" cities, many of the processes in the historical sequence outlined earlier are recurring. These include media sensationalism, an enhanced criminal justice system response,[18] and an effective breakup of solidarity within communities. Times have changed. The fact that more minority members have risen into the middle classes is taken, through a perversion of Wilson's (1978) complex sociological argument, as evidence that race no longer holds people down.

There are still voices of protest even as there were in Los Angeles during the 1940s. Some of these voices echo our recent history. Thus, the Eisenhower Foundation report defines minority youth crime as "a form of slow rioting" that calls for major development efforts within minority communities (Curtis, 1985). It urges that crime prevention in the inner city be viewed not as an end of crime. This is a sophisticated analysis, but it continues to neglect intra-community differentiation.

It seems, therefore, that as welfare state and civil rights initiatives weaken, these intra-community processes become more rather than less important. Furthermore, the history that I have presented suggests that the "tangle of pathology" or the growth of a so-called "underclass" is not a simple process. Nor is it even self-perpetuating.

END NOTES

1. In his own work, Kitsuse is concerned with the "social differentiation of deviants as a process by which others **make** persons different, often independent of whether or not they really are different" (personal communication, April 19, 1985). However, Schur, for one, struggles with "the line between reactions to...perceived deviance [on the one hand] and devaluing responses to racial and ethnic minorities, and to women [on the other hand]" (1984). Being placed in an "other" category is taken by some writers as tantamount to being labeled as deviant, and by Schur as the equivalent of devaluation.

2. James Orcutt has called my attention to the fact that Milton Mankoff (1971) used similar terms — "ascriptive rule breaking" and "achieved rule breaking." However, Mankoff uses "ascriptive rule breaking" to summarize the existing work of labeling theorists with regard to the "physically and visibly handicapped" in a more general critique of the validity of labeling theory for understanding the development of deviant careers. I am interested in the impact of the ascriptive labeling of minority males in general and on minority community treatment of gang members and ex-offenders. Clearly, I am not describing physically handicapped persons. My interest is in processes — in communities where all the members are in jeopardy of labeling — rather than in individual career issues.

3. There is a hint in some of the literature that even the respectable in poor communities tolerate deviance. I have not found that criminality is accepted; rather, the law-abiding minority poor learn that they can rarely count on responsive and fair police work. However, neither is it true that all law-abiding families reject the form of young male deviance that is expressed in barrio gang membership. Minorities cannot be expected to share Anglo moral orders that are closely linked to Anglo stereotypes, i.e., that the neighborhood gang is an inherently criminal phenomenon. Thus, the minority community violates what Kitsuse identifies as one of Goffman's postulates for effective stigmatization: that "those who impose stigma...[share a moral order with] those on whom they are imposed" (Kitsuse, 1980).

4. Parkin (1972), and other English writers on the class structure are extremely useful but are difficult to apply to American class structures, because the concept of race is so important in the United States. Thus, Parkin discusses both radical and accommodationist value sets, but white working class radicals are not the same as protest-oriented minorities.

5. The gang members of the Young Lords and Blackstone Rangers and the ex-convicts of the Black Panthers are well-known, but the mix of Chicano demonstrators is less well known. In the major street protests of Los Angeles on August 29, 1970, the march was led by the striking farmworkers of Cesar Chavez's "Huelguistas." Then came a self-help group of ex-offenders (LUCHA). Next came two traditional middle-class Mexican American political organizations (MAPA and LULAC). Then, the Brown Berets — the Chicano versions of the Young Lords with many gang members — were followed by the staff members of militant publications and by a large group of Chicano college student organizations (Acosta, 1973).

6. Thus, the High Potential program at UCLA, designed to recruit minority students, rapidly became known as the "High Pot" program, permitting the implication that all of these promising minority students were high on pot all the time.

7. I am indebted to Deigo Vigil for his insights into this process in which he participated. It is probable that there were parallels in the black community.

8. This history is derived in part from interviews conducted during a series of studies funded largely by grants from the National Institute on Drug Abuse, especially DAO 3114, and the National Institute of Mental Health, MH 33104. Of course, neither agency is responsible for opinions expressed here.

9. Thus, in one of the barrios that we studied — Hoyo Maravilla — a sheriff's deputy was quoted in 1932, "There is not much we can do to break up the gangs. ... We talk to the boys and take them home and talk to the parents. Some of the parents don't seem to care what their kids do and others lick the tar out of them. ... The kids themselves know that we are not likely to really do anything to them" (Lanigan, 1932-67).

10. One academic who grew up in Los Angeles at the time comments, "Young people of my generation lived on various levels of pachuquismo (acculturation). Everyone, for example, wore drapes or the equivalent for women. Really straight square dress was rare. Mexicans from Mexico wore square clothes upon arrival, but not for long. It was stylish to wear drapes and sharp **calcos** (shoes). But, again, this was the style set by the movies for all American youth. There was a very large element of **'semis,'** i.e. young Chicanos who were stylishly **pachuco** but not extreme. Their language and behavior and such was also 'semi.' The 'semi' operated between **pachuco** culture and **gabacho** (Anglo) society" (Ralph Guzmán, personal communication 1985).

11. In fact, 20 years later, when I began a large-scale study of Mexican Americans, many "respectable" Mexican Americans found it difficult to believe that Anglo liberals could define the zoot-suiters as victims, given the overwhelming effect of the media. Members of our project's community advisory committee urged us not to study marijuana use in the barrios, because it would further stigmatize them. "Square" youth, some of whom are now Chicano professionals, had been ridiculed as **lambion** ("kiss-ass") or had their school lunches or movie money stolen by these same **pachucos** — or had watched barrio fights from a safe distance. But not all gang members were hostile to achievers. As one source notes, "Many squares then and today are protected by gang members. There is much evidence that **pachucos** (then) and cholos (today) exhibit **raza** pride for Chicano achievers" (Ralph Guzmán, personal communication, 1985).

12. In a recent study of a Dallas barrio, Achor (1978) notes a similar situation: "Barrio residents sometimes speak of **los pelados** (poor, wretched people)...but they do not consider them sufficiently numerous to constitute a large and threatening element of the barrio's social world. They usually explain that problem families have suffered severe and prolonged hardship" (1978). Again, "many residents...view their neighborhood as relatively safe...[and] the people...do not seem to fear their neighbors—but many **do** show signs of fearing the police" (1978).

13. Thus, Diego Vigil identified Murietta and Tiburcio Vasquez—bandits of the post-Conquest era—as "Early Chicano Guerilla Fighters" (1974) and dedicated his paper to a man killed in an armed robbery in 1971 as a "modern prototype of a Chicano social bandit" (see also Cortés, 1972). Vigil suggests further that the **Californios** were the accommodationists of their time and reacted to these desperados much as the 1940s accommodationists reacted to their modern counterparts, the gangs.

14. Ramon Salcido (1979) found significant differences in background and attitudes between professionals and paraprofessional gang workers. Most of the paraprofessionals had been affiliated with gangs; most of the professionally trained social workers had not. Paraprofessionals with early gang affiliations had far more complex perceptions of the composition and nature of the gangs. The professionals, trained largely in psychological models, seemed to focus more on individualistic theory-derived views. Paraprofessionals tended to emphasize community intervention; professionals emphasized casework intervention tactics.

15. There was, of course, no more consensus on reintegration than there had been on stigmatization. The tipping of the balance was shown when traditionalist spokespersons protested the formation of a small heroin-detoxification unit in a hospital ward funded by Model Cities. The Mexican-born representative for Model Cities appeared before the city council to denounce the "shameful" fact that an ex-offender group had been involved in this unit and to demand the elimination of the program and the presence of ex-offenders from the overall city planning. She was soundly defeated.

16. This echoed the advice given to the UCLA Mexican American Study Project in the mid-1960s.

17. Evidence from interviews with the parents and siblings of ex-convict gang members shows that in many cases the family as a whole, rather than just the individual lawbreaker, is labeled as criminal and made to feel less comfortable in its neighborhood (Moore and Long, 1981).

18. The rate of juvenile incarceration increased nationally from 167 per 100,000 in 1979 to 184 per 100,000 in 1982. In California it increased from 378 per 100,000 in 1979 to 456 per 100,000 in 1982. As of 1982, 56 percent of adult state and federal prisoners were members of minority groups (U.S. Department of Justice Bureau of Justice Statistics, 1984).

REFERENCES

Achor, S. *Mexican Americans in a Dallas Barrio*. Tucson: University of Arizona Press, 1978, p. 131.

Acosta, O. Z. *The Revolt of the Cockroach People.* San Francisco: Straight Arrow Press, 1973.

Acuna, R. *Occupied America.* New York: Harper and Row, 1981.

Acuna, R. *A Community Under Siege: A Chronicle of Chicanos East of the Los Angeles River, 1945-1975.* Los Angeles: University of California-Los Angeles Chicano Studies Research Center Publications, 1984, pp. 104, 337.

Adams, N. America's newest crime syndicate — the Mexican mafia. *Reader's Digest, 111:* 97-102, 1977.

Banfield, E. *The Unheavenly City.* New York: Little, Brown, 1970.

Bogardus, E. S. *The City Boy and His Problems: A Survey of Boy Life in Los Angeles.* Rotary Club, 1926.

Burma, J. *Spanish-Speaking Groups in the United States.* Durham, NC: Duke University Press, 1954.

Cortes, C. "The Chicano Social Bandit as Romantic Hero." Unpublished paper, 1972.

Curtis, L. (Ed.). *American Violence and Public Policy.* New Haven: Yale University Press, 1985, p.8.

Drake, St. C. and Cayton, H. *Black Metropolis.* New York: Harper and Row, 1962, p.661 (originally published 1945).

Goffman, E. *Stigma.* Englewood Cliffs, NJ: Prentice-Hall, 1963, p.4.

Gonzalez, A. "Mexican/Chicano Gangs in Los Angeles: A Sociohistorical Case Study." Ph.D. Dissertation, University of California-Berkeley, 1982.

Griffith, B. *American Me.* Boston: Houghton Mifflin, 1948.

Kitsuse, J. Coming out all over: deviants and the politics of social problems. *Social Problems, 28:*1-13, 1980.

Lanigan, M. "Second Generation Mexicans in Belvedere." M.A. Thesis, University of Southern California, 1932.

McWilliams, C. *North from Mexico.* New York: Greenwood Press, 1949.

Maldonado, L., and Moore, J. *Changing Urban Ethnicity: New Immigrants and Old Minorities.* Beverly Hills: Sage, 1985.

Mankoff, M. Societal reaction and career deviance: a critical analysis. *Sociological Quarterly, 12:*204-18, 1971.

Matza, D. "The Disreputable Poor," in R. Bendix and S.M. Lipset (Eds.): *Class, Status and Power.* New York: The Free Press, 1966.

Mazon, M. "Social Upheaval in World War II: 'Zoot-suiters' and Servicemen in Los Angeles, 1943." Ph.D. Dissertation, University of California-Los Angeles, 1976.

Moore, J., Garcia, R., Garcia, C., Cerda, L., and Valencia, F. *A Model for Chicano Drug Use and for Effective Utilization of Employment and Training Resources by Barrio Addicts and Ex-Offenders.* Los Angeles: Chicano Pinto Research Project, 1979.

Moore, J. W., and Long, J. *Barrio Impact of High Incarceration Rates.* Los Angeles: Chicano Pinto Research Project, 1981.

Moynihan, D. P. "The Negro Family: The Case of National Action," in L. Rainwater and W. L. Yancy (Eds.): *The Moynihan Report and the Politics of Controversy.* Cambridge, M.I.T. Press, 1967.

Office of Juvenile Justice and Delinquency Prevention. *Police Handling of Gangs.* Washington, D.C.: National Juvenile Justice Assessment Center, 1983.

Parkin, F. *Class Inequality and the Political Order.* New York: Praeger, 1972, p. 81.

Redfield, R. *Folk Culture of Yucatan.* Chicago: University of Chicago Press, 1941, p. 28.

Rubel, A. The Mexican American palomilla. *Anthropological Linguistics, 4*:29-97, 1965.

Salcido, R. "Gang Workers," in J. Moore, R. Salcido, D. Vigil and R. Garcia: *A Model for Chicano Drug Use and for Effective Utilization of Employment and Training Resources by Barrio Addicts and Ex-Offenders.* Los Angeles: Chicano Pinto Research Project, 1979, pp. 126-137.

Schur, E. *Labeling Women Deviant: Gender, Stigma and Social Control.* New York: Random House, U.S. Department of Justice, Bureau of Justice Statistics, 1984.

Schur, E. *Prisoners in State and Federal Institutions on December 31, 1982.* Washington, D.C.: U.S. Department of Justice, 1984.

Vigil, D. *Early Chicano Guerilla Fighters.* Upland, CA: JDB Publications, 1974.

Vigil, D. "Street Youth in Mexican American Barrios." Unpublished manuscript, 1985a.

Vigil, D. Chicano gangs: one response to Mexican urban adaptation in the Los Angeles area. *Urban Anthropology, 12*:45-75, 1985b.

Warner, W. L., and Lunt, P. "The Stigmatization Process," in D. Wilkinson and R. Taylor (Eds.): *The Black Male of America.* Chicago: Nelson-Hall, 1977.

Wilson, W. J. *The Declining Significance of Race.* Chicago: University of Chicago Press, 1978.

CHAPTER 6

THE CHICANO AND THE LAW: AN ANALYSIS OF COMMUNITY-POLICE CONFLICT IN AN URBAN BARRIO

ALFREDO MIRANDÉ

THE RISING rate of crime and urban unrest in the late 1960s led to an overwhelming concern not only with issues of crime and civil disorders but with official violence and the violation of civil liberties. Of particular interest was whether fear of crime increased support for police power and decreased support for civil liberties. Much of the research that emerged in the aftermath of these urban disorders focused either on the evaluation of the police services by black respondents or on racial differences in perceptions of the police and crime (e.g. Smith and Hawkins, 1973; Furstenberg and Wellford, 1973; Phillips and Coates, 1971; Chackerian and Barrett, 1973; Hahn, 1971). Such studies showed that black respondents were consistently more negative in their evaluation of the police (Bayley and Mendelsohn, 1969; Ennis, 1967; Raine, 1970; Hahn, 1971; Furstenberg and Wellford, 1973), and that negative attitudes were not limited to lower-status respondents but might in fact be more intense among persons of higher status[1] (Murphy and Watson, 1970; Raine, 1970). Although these studies provided useful insights into minority-police relations, their almost exclusive focus on blacks resulted in the neglect of perceptions of the police and crime held by other minority group members. There has been, in particular, very little research on Chicano perceptions of the police or relations with them.

The U.S. Commission on Civil Rights, in perhaps the most systematic and far-reaching study of Chicanos and the legal and judicial system, found strong evidence of a pattern of systematic harassment and abuse of Chicanos by the police. The commission concluded that "Mexican American citizens are subject to unduly harsh treatment by law enforcement officers, that they are often arrested on insufficient grounds, receive physical and verbal abuse, and penalties which are disproportionately severe" (1970). Although patterns of police abuse and mistreatment are common and widespread,[2] the study of Chicano-police relations has been neglected by sociologists. There is a need for research that examines the attitudes of barrio residents toward law enforcement not only during major incidents but in their day-to-day contact with police. This study attempts to add to our understanding of Chicano-police relations by presenting an overview of conflict with police in an urban barrio, testing several hypotheses concerning fear of the police, attitudes toward increasing or curtailing police power, support of civil liberties, and fear of crime. For example, do barrio residents blame the police for major disturbances in the community, or are they basically supportive of police? Does support for increasing police power increase as fear of crime increases? Does fear of the police by Chicanos lead to greater support for civil liberties and increase the desire to curtail police power as is the case in other racial-ethnic groups?

THE SETTING

The setting for this case study of Chicano-police conflict is a barrio in a Southern California community of 150,000 inhabitants. This barrio was selected not only because it has been the site of recent civil disorders which have gained national attention, but because it appeared representative of other barrios in the Southwest in being isolated from Anglo society and having a long history of conflict with the police. Like most barrios, it is a distinctive community within the city, extending over an area that is approximately one square mile and includes about 3,000 persons within its boundaries.

From its inception as housing quarters for citrus pickers, the community has been segregated from the city. As early as 1874 the City Board of Education created a separate school district to exclude Chicano children from Anglo schools. Since there were not many Chicano residents in the 1880s and 1890s, the area became an Anglo suburb and was the site of several exclusive social clubs, a tennis club, and a polo club. But segregation prevailed, and within 25 years the suburb was transformed into a Chicano barrio surrounded by large, prestigious homes. Problems with the law surfaced early. In 1916 a citizen's committee chaired by the mayor requested and obtained the hiring of extra policemen for the barrio, and the following year an extra officer was hired to patrol on Saturday nights. In the same year requests were made for as many as eight additional policemen. Since the 1940s killings, shootings and beatings of Chicanos have been commonplace.

The barrio shares certain important features with urban slums in that the income and educational level of many residents is low and some of the housing is poor or substandard, but it differs from the slum in some important respects. First, although there is poverty in the barrio, not everyone is poor. There is considerable variability in the economic and educational attainment of residents.[3] Second, the barrio has emerged partly as a result of prejudice and segregation but there is an element of voluntarism in barrio residence, and a strong sense of community identification prevails. Barrios are literally colonias (colonies), ethnic enclaves within the territorial boundaries of the United States.

This particular barrio is similarly isolated. Its isolation has been so extensive that until recent years many of the streets in the barrio were unpaved and residents were not afforded normal city services. Today, ambulances are still reluctant to enter the community without a police escort.

The confluence of two diverse though mutually reinforcing forces — residential segregation and a positive identification with barrio residence — have worked to produce a remarkably stable pattern of community residence. Not only are most residents of the community Chicano (about 90%), but typically they have lived there all or virtually all of their lives. This does not necessarily mean that most people born and raised in the barrio remain there for the rest of their lives, since a community survey obviously excludes those persons who have moved out. What is significant is not that most people who are born in the barrio stay there but that very few new residents move in. New arrivals, especially if they come from Mexico, are likely to have relatives or friends already in the community. The stability of the community is further intensified by what appears to be a tendency toward endogamous marriage, so that a strong sense of familism pervades community life. The statement frequently made in jest that "everyone in the barrio is related to everyone else" is not without some factual basis. One person, for example, noted that he had over 260 relatives living in the community.

The stability, cohesiveness, and apparent serenity of the community stand in sharp contrast to the conflict and tension that pervades community-police relations. The police have traditionally been viewed not only as outsiders but as representatives of the dominant oppressive Anglo society. Over the past seven or eight years there has been about one Chicano shot per year. Residents complain of extensive police abuse and harassment. Community-police conflict is especially intense among youth, who are frequently the target of such abuse and harassment.

Community-police conflict culminated in two major incidents in August 1975. One incident occurred on August second where the police broke up a bachelor party, tear gassed the home where the party was held, and beat up and arrested a large number of the guests. Although 52 persons were arrested, almost all charges were subsequently dropped for insufficient evidence, and the city has since settled a number of civil suits out of court. The second incident was unrelated but served to exacerbate antipolice sentiment. The stabbing of an Anglo male believed to be a police informer, at a park in the community on August thirteenth, provided the impetus for this incident. The police, in pursuit of the assailant(s), surrounded a cornfield throughout the evening of August thirteenth and the morning of August fifteenth. Tear gas was dropped from a helicopter, and there was extensive gunfire throughout the night. Sheriff's units from the county and a nearby county were brought in to reinforce city police, as was the SWAT team from San Diego. The result was a police siege. Residents were stopped and questioned by police as they attempted to go to work or carry on normal daily activities. The August thirteenth incident was termed a riot by the police and the media. If it was a "riot," it was more of the "commodity" than the "communal" variety, although there was no looting or destruction of business property. It was more accurately a community-police confrontation, with the police intermittently exchanging gunfire with residents.

HYPOTHESES, METHOD, AND SAMPLE

Our survey of community attitudes toward the police was carried out within two months of these incidents. Its primary objective was to assess attitudes toward the police not only relative to their handling of the August incidents but in general. The interview schedule covered a number of areas, including: (1) general attitudes concerning the police, protection of civil liberties, and fear of crime; (2) specific attitudes toward the police and their handling of the August incidents; and (3) social and demographic characteristics.

Given the putative extensiveness of police abuse and widespread official violence perpetrated against Chicanos, there is need for research that focuses on the conditions under which Chicanos are willing either to increase or to curtail police power and to support or not support civil liberties. Several hypotheses tested by Block (1971) in an NORC study were tested with our barrio respondents. While the hypotheses were originally tested with white and black respondents, they seem especially applicable to Chicanos. One hypothesis proposes that since fear provides a rationale for granting the state power, fear of crime should lead to greater support for increasing police power. A second hypothesis similarly argues that if fear is the primary basis for delimiting the power of the state, then fear of the police should intensify support for civil liberties. The rationale for these hypotheses, according to Block (1974), is as follows:

> If fear is a foundation of support for the state and the police are the state's instrument to control internal threat, then those people with the greatest fear of crime should be most willing to increase the power of the police. Similarly if fear of the state is the basis for limitation of the power of the state, and the police, as an instrument of the state, are a basis of fear of the state, then those respondents who most fear the police would be most likely to want their power limited through the protection of civil liberties. (Pp. 93-94)

In applying these hypotheses to Chicanos we expected that while barrio residents would not generally support increasing police power, those who feared crime most would be most willing to support such increases. Also, since police abuse and brutality entail the violation of civil liberties, we expected widespread support for such safeguards and considerable fear of the police, but support of civil liberties should be especially high among respondents who are most fearful of the police. We hypothesized, finally, that those barrio respondents who were most fearful of the police would want not only to protect civil liberties but to curtail or limit police power.

A random sample of households yielded 170 complete interviews. Though the sample is based on a random selection of households, it is somewhat purposive in the sense that a special effort was made to include youthful respondents, since it is among them that conflict with the police is believed to be most intense. Interviewers were instructed to interview an adult member of the household and a teenaged member whenever possible. This procedure was facilitated by interviewers normally working as two-person teams. Inclusion of youth was deemed important also, because Chicanos as a group are on the average much younger than the overall population.[4] The sample consists of 38 percent male adults, 35 percent female adults, 16 percent male teenagers, and 9 percent female teenagers. Approximately one out of every four respondents then is a dependent child.

Interviews were conducted by bilingual-bicultural interviewers, trained and sensitive to the nuances of Chicano culture and the prevailing values of the barrio. Comments and suggestions of various political, civic, and community leaders were sought and incorporated into the interview schedule. Interviewers and the principal investigator met with these leaders and were briefed on practices, procedures, dress, and demeanor that were believed would elicit maximum cooperation from the community in carrying out the project. Without the help and endorsement of these community members, our task would have been difficult, if not impossible.

Basically, the same questions used in the NORC survey were included as measures of the four major test variables in the study. Fear of crime was measured by the question:

> **How likely is it that a person walking around here at night might be held up or attacked — very likely, somewhat likely, somewhat unlikely, or very unlikely?**

The index of fear of the police was the person's perception of "police respectfulness toward people like himself." Those respondents who rated police respectfulness as "not so good" were assumed to fear the police more than those who rated it as "pretty good" or "very good." In order to assess support for increases in police power respondents were asked:

> **Do you favor giving the police more power to question people, do you think they have enough power already, or would you like to see some of their power to question people curtailed?**

The last variable, protection of civil liberties, was measured by two questions regarding support for police review boards and for the right of a suspect to an attorney during police interrogations. Respondents who felt that a suspect has a right to a lawyer and who were in favor of establishing a police review board were said to have "full support" of civil liberties.

FINDINGS

Attitudes Towards Police and Their Handling of the Incidents

A number of open and closed questions were used to ascertain respondent perception of the August incidents and the police handling of them. In response to an item that asked "What do you see as the major reasons for the August Second incident?" few respondents blamed the youth at the bachelor party, and most specified police overreaction as the major factor leading to the disturbance. Significantly, 57 percent felt that the police overreacted a great deal and used force and violence which were not needed. Most respondents felt that the August second incident could have been avoided (59%), some felt that it could not (14%), and some either did not know for sure or did not answer (26%). Those who felt it could have been avoided were asked to indicate how it could have been avoided. The most common response was that it could have been avoided had the police used better judgment or not overreacted, at least indirectly blaming the August second incident on the police.

Our barrio residents were similarly critical of the police handling of the August thirteenth incident. In response to an open-ended question on reasons for this disturbance, 41 percent said they did not know, while the majority of those who responded saw poor judgment and overreaction by the police as major reasons for the disturbance. Most persons who responded also felt that the August thirteenth incident could have been avoided if the police had handled the situation better and if they would stop overpatrolling and harassment of residents.

In a broader light, a series of open-ended questions asked respondents to indicate what they saw as the most important reasons for conflict between the community and city police as a whole. Although a variety of reasons were given, by far the most common one given for community-police conflict (35%) was police prejudice, harassment, and overpatrolling. Another open-ended question asked what they saw as the best way to solve the problem of barrio-police conflict. Although 47 percent did not offer any solution, most who did specified a need either to improve communication with the police or to reform them, and few blamed the community for the problem.

The final open-ended question asked how the city police department could improve its services "to you, your neighbors, and community" and provided an interesting diversity of results. The responses ranged from those that felt the police were "doing a good job" or "needed to enforce the law more" to those who felt that the "situation was hopeless" or that the police should "leave us alone"; intermediate between these extremes were persons who simply wanted to improve police services. A substantial number called for the police to treat them with "respect" or "like humans" and to have more "understanding" of barrio residents.

While it is clear from the preceding that most respondents were critical of the police handling of the August incidents and saw their mishandling of these incidents as part of a broader pattern of pervasive police harassment and abuse, their negativity was neither all-encompassing nor predictable. In order to obtain a more direct measure of perceptions of community-police conflict, respondents were asked to "rate relations between police and residents of the barrio" on a five-point scale ranging from excellent to poor. Only 1 percent rated relations between the police and community as excellent, and 48 percent rated them as poor.

Though relations between the police and the community are rated very low, barrio residents are not uniformly critical of the police. When they were asked to give the police department an overall rating, it was rated higher than were relations between the police and the community. Yet, more persons rated the department as below average or poor than rated it as good or excellent. Differences between the rating of the police department per se and rating of relations between them and the community suggest considerable sophistication on the part of barrio residents and a keen awareness of differential treatment toward them by police. Chicanos do not tend to see the police as ill-trained or inept as much as they see them as treating them differently and unequally relative to others. A common complaint expressed by barrio residents is not that they want special or unusual treatment, only equal treatment with others.

Fear of Crime and Support for the Police in the Barrio

The preceding description suggests that Chicano dissatisfaction was relatively specific and not generalized to all situations. Not only did Chicano perceptions of the police vary across situations, but there was considerable diversity among them in their perceptions and evaluations of the police. A number of barrio residents were, in fact, supportive of the police and in some instances felt that they should be granted more power to deal with crime and quell disturbances. Let us now examine certain conditions that may be associated with a willingness to increase police power and limit civil liberties. The questions are worded more broadly, so rather than eliciting specific attitudes toward a given police department or actual incidents, they tap more general and abstract attitudes.

The first hypothesis posits that fear of crime among barrio residents is translated into a greater willingness to support increases in police power. It must initially be noted that fear of crime in the barrio appears to be minimal. Only 23 percent feel that attack in their neighborhood is "very likely," while 28 percent see it as "very unlikely." As expected, few respondents want to increase police power and many wish either to curtail or to limit police power to its current level. Thirty-two percent wish to curtail police power and only about 14 percent wish to increase it from its current level.

From Table 1 it is clear that the hypothesis is supported in this sample. Those barrio residents who say street attack is very likely are more likely to favor increases in police power. Eighteen percent of the respondents who believe attack is very likely support increasing police power, whereas only 4 percent of those who feel it is very unlikely do so. Chicanos who see attack as very unlikely, on the other hand, are much more inclined to want to curtail police power (54%) than those who see attack as very likely (26%).

Table 1 also shows the effect of several important background variables on the relationship between fear of crime and support for the police. Age appears to affect this relationship. That the relationship is strongest among barrio residents under 25 is perhaps not surprising, since it is Chicano youth who more typically have direct experience with both crime and the police.

Two important patterns are evident when length of residence in the community is considered. First and most obvious is the great stability of residence among our respondents; only about 13 percent have lived in the community for less that five years, whereas 29 percent have lived there from five to fifteen years and 58 percent for sixteen or more. Second, the relationship between fear of crime and support for the police is not as strong or significant among short-term residents, among whom the relationship is inverse, although not significant. Apparently, among short-term residents those who fear crime most are least supportive of the police. Length of residence in the barrio seems to enhance identification with the community and to intensify the relation between fear of crime and support of the police.

Table 1

SUPPORT FOR THE POLICE AND FEAR OF ATTACK

Support Police	Fear of Attack			
	Very Likely	Somewhat Likely	Somewhat Unlikely	Very Unlikely
More	18%	18%	19%	4%
Enough	55	69	45	41
Curtail	26	12	35	54
Total	100%	100%	100%	100%
N	38	49	31	46

Gamma = .35, Chi Square = 22.42, P < .001

Support for the Police by Fear of Attack Controlling for*:

	Gamma	Chi Square	P <	N
1. *Age*				
24 or less	.60	5.91	.05	44
25-40	.22	.52	.77	39
41 or more	.31	2.28	.31	43
2. *Length of Residence*				
Less than 5 years	−.38	.90	.64	21
5-15 years	.55	10.42	.005	46
16 years or more	.58	11.01	.005	93
3. *Like Living in Community*				
Yes	.58	15.04	.001	114
No	−.12	.19	.91	47
4. *Sex*				
Male	.71	18.01	.001	89
Female	.06	2.08	.35	75
5. *Family Income*				
Under $7,000	.58	4.68	.10	39
$7,000-$9,999	.21	4.16	.12	30
$10,000 or more	.11	.32	.85	35
6. *Education*				
8 years or less	.68	8.65	.01	34
Some high school	.19	.82	.66	30
12 years or more	.44	3.94	.14	46

*Because of the small N's, Fear of Attack was dichotomized into "Likely" and "Unlikely."

A related control variable is whether the resident is satisfied living in the community or is dissatisfied and would like to move. The hypothesis is much more strongly supported among persons who like living in the barrio. It may well be that community identification increases involvement with community issues such as crime and control of the police so that the relationship between these variables is most intense among those who identify with and are committed to the barrio.

The effect of gender on fear of crime and support for the police is clear and predictable. Since males in the barrio typically have more direct contact and exposure to crime and to the police, it may be expected that the relationship between these variables is much stronger among men than among women. The extent to which women in the barrio fear crime is less likely to affect their attitudes toward either increasing or curtailing police power.

The effects of income and education are less clear, but the relationship between fear of crime and support for increasing police power is strongest among respondents with low incomes and little formal education. Chicanos with low incomes and little schooling, like men and youth in the barrio, are more likely to be victims of crime and of police abuse.

Fear of the Police and Support for Civil Liberties in the Barrio

The second major hypothesis concerns the effects of fear of the police on support for civil liberties among barrio residents. My hypothesis is that those Chicanos who are most fearful of police tend to be more supportive of civil guarantees, since such guarantees are designed to limit police abuses. Table 2 shows that the relationship is in the predicted direction but not statistically significant.

Approximately 70 percent of those Chicanos who fear the police most support both measures to protect civil liberties compared to only 50 percent of those who fear the police least. The lack of statistical significance is undoubtedly due at least in part to the overall level of commitment to civil liberties among the Chicanos in our sample.[5] There was, in fact, little variation in the dependent variable, given that none was opposed to both measures and 82 percent supported both measures.[6] In view of the level of support for civil liberties among barrio respondents, it may not be considered surprising to find substantial fear of police among them. Approximately 39 percent rated police respect towards persons like themselves as "not so good," and only 22 percent rated it as "very good."

Table 2

SUPPORT FOR CIVIL LIBERTIES AND FEAR OF THE POLICE

Support Civil Liberties	Police Respect		
	Very Good	Pretty Good	Not So Good
Less Support	50%	38%	30%
Full Support	50	62	71
Total	100%	100%	100%
N	34	60	61

Gamma = .27, Chi Square = 3.95, P < .14

Support for Civil Liberties and Fear of the Police Controlling for*:

	Gamma	Chi Square	P <	N
1. *Age*				
24 or less	.21	.11	.73	43
25-40	.50	1.16	.28	36
41 or more	.03	.09	.76	39
2. *Length of Residence*				
Less than 5 years	−.41	—	.41**	21
5-15	.38	.79	.37	44
16 years or more	.35	1.98	.16	88
3. *Like Living in Community*				
Yes	.27	1.31	.25	111
No	.14	0.00	1.00	42
4. *Sex*				
Male	.14	.13	.72	87
Female	.09	0.00	1.00	68
5. *Family Income*				
Under $7,000	.08	.02	.90	38
$7,000-$9,999	1.00	—	.04**	28
$10,000 or more	0.00	.15	.70	33
6. *Education*				
8 years or less	.09	—	.62**	30
Some high school	.41	—	.26**	30
12 years or more	.20	.10	.75	45

*Because of the small N's the "Very Good" and "Pretty Good" response to Police Respect were combined into a single "Good" category.
**Based on Fisher's Exact Probability Test.

The relationship between fear of the police and support for civil liberties appears stronger among Chicanos who are 25-40 years of age than among younger or older ones, and when age is dichotomized it is considerably stronger among those 30 or older than among those under 30. Perhaps the reason for this is that the relationship between fear of the police and support for civil liberties is more indirect and abstract than the relationship between fear of crime and support for increasing police power, thereby manifesting itself more clearly among older or more mature barrio residents.

The hypothesis is more strongly supported among long-term residents of the community. In fact, among short-term residents the relationship is in the opposite direction; those Chicanos who fear the police most are least supportive of civil liberties. Although not statistically significant, there is also slightly more support for the hypothesis among those who like living in the barrio than those who do not, men than women, Chicanos of moderate rather than low or high income, and those with moderate rather than low or high educational attainment.

Fear of the Police and Support for the Police in the Barrio

The preceding hypotheses have been based on the assumption that much of the willingness of barrio residents to increase police power and limit civil guarantees is grounded in fear, both of crime and of the police. Fear of crime is likely to lead some residents of the barrio to support increasing the power of the police. Fear of the police, on the other hand, intensifies the support of civil liberties, thereby limiting police abuses. Just as fear of the police should lead to greater support for civil liberties, so should it increase the desire to limit the power of police in the barrio, a hypothesis that will now be examined.

From Table 3 it is clear that the relationship between fear of the police and support for the police is strong and significant among our barrio respondents. As predicted, those Chicanos who fear the police most are least likely to support increases in police power. Of the respondents who fear the police, 63 percent (i.e. who see police respect toward people like themselves as "not so good") desire to curtail or to limit police power, whereas only 9 percent of those who do not fear the police desire to curtail it.

From Table 3 it is also clear that the relationship between fear of the police and support for limiting police power remains significant even

Table 3

SUPPORT FOR THE POLICE AND FEAR OF THE POLICE

| | Police Respect | | |
Support Police	Very Good	Pretty Good	Not So Good
More	32%	20%	2%
Enough	59	67	35
Curtail	9	13	63
Total	100%	100%	100%
N	34	61	60

Gamma = .72, Chi Square = 51.84, P < .001

Support for the Police and Fear of the Police*:

	Gamma	Chi Square	P	N
1. *Age*				
24 or less	.74	10.06	.01	43
25-40	.94	14.25	.001	36
41 or more	.63	5.19	.07	40
2. *Length of Residence*				
Less than 5 years	1.00	9.29	.01	20
5-15	.98	29.39	.001	45
16 years or more	.73	18.10	.001	88
3. *Like Living in Community*				
Yes	.84	35.83	.001	111
No	.89	9.88	.01	42
4. *Sex*				
Male	.95	38.35	.001	88
Female	.65	9.60	.01	67
5. *Family Income*				
Under $7,000	.91	13.38	.001	39
$7,000-$9,999	.95	12.61	.001	28
$10,000 or more	.71	11.15	.005	33
6. *Education*				
8 years or less	.96	13.71	.001	30
Some high school	.56	3.21	.20	30
12 years or more	.92	11.69	.005	45

*Because of the small N's the "Very Good" and "Pretty Good" responses to Police Respect were combined into a single "Good" category.

when background variables are controlled. The relationship cuts across age groups in the barrio, although it appears weaker among older respondents. It is similarly supported among newly arrived and long-term residents, those who like living in the community as well as those who wish to move out of the barrio, men and women, persons of low, moderate, and high income, and across educational groups, although it is not significant among Chicanos with "some high school" education.

SUMMARY AND DISCUSSION

This is a case study of a Southern California barrio that, like many others in the Southwest, has a tradition of conflict with the police. Several hypotheses were tested concerning fear of crime and of the police and support for increasing or curtailing police power and protecting civil liberties.

The hypothesis that fear of crime leads to increases in support for police power, a hypothesis which received only moderate support in the NORC study, was strongly supported by our Chicano respondents. This suggests that the view of Chicanos as uniformly antipolice and supportive of crime should be modified and take into account the diversity of attitudes found among them. There appears to be a significant segment of the barrio who are fearful of crime and seek to increase police power. While it would be wrong to characterize them as a "silent majority," since most barrio residents feel that the police already have enough power and many more wish to curtail than to increase police power, there is a need to acknowledge the existence of this segment of the Chicano community. It is noteworthy that the hypothesis is more strongly supported among those who are more involved with both crime and the police (e.g. men, youth).

The second hypothesis—that Chicanos who fear the police most are most likely to favor the protection of civil liberties—received only limited support in our survey, substantial support among whites, and virtually none among blacks in the NORC survey. One reason for the relatively weak support for the hypothesis among Chicanos was their almost universal approval of civil liberties. More than four of five Chicanos supported both forms of civil liberties, discussed at the end of the section entitled "Hypotheses, Method, and Sample," compared to six of ten blacks and only three of ten whites in the NORC survey who supported both. The almost universal support of civil liberties among Chicanos suggests a need for discarding prevailing measures of civil liberties in favor of more sophisticated ones capable of discerning possible intra-group differences in such support.

The final relationship examined was fear of the police and support for increased police power. There was very strong support for the hypothesis that fear of the police among barrio residents increases the desire to curtail police power. As significant as the magnitude of the relationship was the fact that it generally held across age groups, long, medium and short-term residents of the barrio, Chicanos who liked living in the community and those who did not, men and women, persons of low, moderate and high income, and those of varying educational levels. The strength of this relationship is perhaps not surprising when one considers the history of conflict between Chicanos and the police. As victims of police harassment and abuse, Chicanos have sought to limit and control police power, and much of the desire to curtail their power is grounded in fear of the police and their excesses.

Differences between our findings and those of the NORC study appear consistent with historical differences among the three racial-ethnic groups in attitudes toward crime, treatment by the police and their relationship to the legal-judicial system. Anglos obviously receive better treatment from the police and are more supportive of them than are blacks or Chicanos. They also have less reason to be fearful of personal attack, since they are less apt to be victims of violent crime. Predictably, then, fear of crime is least among white and greatest among black respondents. It is interesting that though Chicanos fear crime less than blacks, they appear to fear the police more. This fear is not without justification. The history of Chicano-police relations has been one of conflict and tension, as has been noted. The police have traditionally served as tools for maintaining not only the oppressed position of Chicanos in the Southwest but their spatial and cultural isolation as well. The police are viewed by Chicanos as a vehicle for perpetuating the interests of Anglo-American society rather than as a supportive or protective agency.

The findings of this study suggest that even among a group of people such as Chicanos, who have been subjected to systematic police abuse and harassment, increases in the crime rate generally lead to greater support for increasing police power and limiting civil liberties, while fear of the police reduces support for police power and increases support for civil guarantees. Because our study is limited to a single barrio in Southern California, these results must be interpreted with caution. Although the barrio appears typical of many other barrios in the Southwest, we cannot be certain the same patterns would be found in other regions, in rural settings, or among non-barrio Chicanos. Before our generalizations are accepted as conclusive, research is needed in other settings. Such research will, I hope, provide additional insights into the dynamics of community-police relations among minority groups and in the population as a whole.

END NOTES

1. Household surveys, however, tend to exclude those persons who are most critical of the police — lower-class young adult black males. A comparison of black street and household respondents found that "the pattern found in previous surveys, suggesting a negative relationship between social status and attitudes of blacks toward police, as indexed by rating of police service, was not supported when the street population was taken into account" (Boggs and Galliher, 1975).

2. From the signing of the Treaty of Guadalupe-Hildalgo to the present, a dual standard of justice has existed in the Southwest for Anglos, on the one hand, and for Chicanos, on the other. Not only has the legal and judicial system been used to perpetuate the economic, political, and social oppression of the Mexican-American people, but also the police have served as a domestic military force to quell disturbances and maintain order in the barrio. The relation between the police and barrio residents has been characterized by distrust, resentment, open hostility, and violence. Rather than diminishing, Chicano-police conflict appears to have intensified (MALDEF, 1978). Many of the riots of the 1940s (Alder, 1974; Endore, 1942; Sleepy Lagoon Defense Committee, 1942) were "communal" riots involving direct confrontations between racial-ethnic groups (Janowitz, 1969), whereas most so-called Chicanos riots today are "commodity" riots and entail a direct confrontation with the police. There is still considerable hostility and conflict directed at Chicanos, but more and more it is expressed indirectly via the police and the courts. (For documentation of police abuse and mistreatment of Chicanos, see U.S. Commission on Civil Rights, 1970; Hoffman, 1974; McWilliams, 1949, 1968; Acuna, 1972; Castillo and Camarillo, 1973; Goldfinch, 1949; Gomez-Q, 1970; Rosenbaum, 1973; Schlesinger, 1971; Trujillo, 1974; Morales, 1972; Adler, 1974; Paredes, 1958; Sleepy Lagoon Defense Committee, 1942; Webb, 1965, 1975; and MALDEF, 1978a & b).

3. The median income in 1970 of all families residing in the census tract where the barrio is located was $6,520 and more than 21 percent of the families were below the poverty level. Approximately 30 percent of the families had incomes below $5000, more than $5,000 but less than $10,000 (47%), between $10,000 and $24,999 (18%), and $25,000 or more (4%). The incomes of our respondents were fairly comparable to the census figures, although a smaller proportion of upper-income families ($25,000 or more) was represented in our sample. About 27 percent of our respondents had incomes under $5,000, between $5,000 and $9,999 (41%), $10,000 to $24,999 (32%), and $25,000 or more (1%). The discrepancy in the proportion of high-income families may have resulted from the fact that the census tract in which

the barrio is located contains a number of affluent Anglo residences that are on the fringe of the barrio in the prestigious Green Belt area. The educational attainment of barrio residents is also low. The median years of school completed for persons 25 years old and over residing in the census tract was 8.4 (compared to 11.0 for the city as a whole), and the proportion who had graduated from high school was 18.4 (compared to 42.5 for the city as a whole). The level of educational attainment was higher in our sample, because persons under 25 are included and younger Chicanos have higher educational attainment. The proportion of high school graduates was 43.9 in our sample.

4. The median age for persons of Mexican origin living in the United States was 20.3 years compared to a median age of 28.9 years for the population as a whole (U.S. Bureau of Census, 1976:1).

5. It should be noted that the measure of support for civil liberties shown in Table 2 among Chicanos is a conservative estimate of such support, since persons whose response in these questions was "not sure" were treated as though they were not in support of civil liberties. In other words, responses were grouped into those who supported civil liberties and those who definitely did not or were not sure. When "not sure" responses are excluded, the hypothesis is more strongly supported but is still not statistically significant.

6. The figure that 82 percent of the respondents support both measures of civil liberties is obtained when "not sure" responses are excluded. When "not sure" responses are included in the computation, the percentage supporting both measures is 63.

REFERENCES

Acuna, R. *Occupied America: The Chicano's Struggle Toward Liberation*. New York: Harper & Row, 1972.

Adler, P. R. "The 1943 Zoot-Suit Riots: Brief Episode in a Long Conflict," in M. P. Servin (Ed.): *An Awakened Minority: The Mexican-Americans*. Encino, CA: Glencoe, 1974, pp. 142-158.

Bayley, D. H., and Mendelsohn, H. *Minorities and the Police*. New York: Macmillan, 1969.

Blocks, R. L. Fear of crime and fear of the police. *Social Problems*, 19(Summer):91-101, 1971.

Boggs, S. L., and Galliher, J. F. Evaluating the police: a comparison of black street and household respondents. *Social Problems*, 11(February):393-416, 1975.

Castillo, P., and Camarillo, A. *Furia y Muerte; Los Bandidos Chicanos*. Los Angeles: Aztlan, 1973.

Chackerian, R., and Barrett, R. F. Police professionalism and citizen evaluation. *Urban Affairs O*, 6(March):345-349, 1973.

Endore, G. *The Sleepy Lagoon Mystery*. Los Angeles: Citizens' Committee for the Defense of Mexican-American Youth, 1942.

Ennis, P. H. *Crime Victimization in the United States: A Report of a National Survey*. Washington, D.C.: U. S. Government Printing Office, 1967.

Furstenberg, F. F., Jr., and Wellford, C. F. Calling the police: the evaluation of police service. *Law and Society Rev*, (Spring):393-406, 1973.

Goldfinch, C. W. "Juan N. Cortina, 1824-1892: A re-appraisal." Master's thesis, University of Chicago, 1949.

Gomez, O. J. Plan de San Diego reviewed. Aztlan: *Chicano J. of Social Sciences and Arts*, *1*(Spring):124-132, 1970.

Hahn, H. Ghetto assessments of police protection and authority. *Law and Society Rev*, *6*(November):183-194, 1971.

Hoffman, A. *Unwanted Mexican-Americans in the Great Depression*. Tucson: University of Arizona Press, 1974.

Janowitz, M. "Patterns of collective racial violence," in H. D. Graham and I. R. Gurr (Eds.): *The History of Violence in America: Historical Comparative Perspective*. New York: Praeger, 1969.

McWilliams, C. California and the wetback. *Common Ground*, *9*(Summer):15-20, 1949.

McWilliams, C. *North from Mexico*. New York: Greenwood, 1968.

Mexican-American Legal Defense and Education Fund (MALDEF). "MALDEF documents official abuse of authority against Mexican-Americans in letter to Attorney General Griffin Bell." San Francisco, 1978a.

Mexican-American Legal Defense and Education Fund (MALDEF). Dallas brutality conference displays Chicano unity. *MALDEF*, *8*(Summer):1-8, 1978b.

Morales, A. *Ando Sangrando [I am Bleeding]: A Study of Mexican-American Police Conflict*. La Puente, CA: Perspective, 1972.

Murphy, R. J., and Watson, J. W. "The Structure of Discontent: Relationship Between Social Structure, Grievance, and Riot Support," in N. Cohen (Ed.): *The Los Angeles Riots*. New York: New York Press, 1970, pp. 140-257.

Paredes, A. *With His Pistol in His Hand: A Border Ballad and Its Hero*. Austin: University of Texas Press, 1958.

Phillips, J. L., and Coates, R. B. Two scales for measuring attitudes toward police. *Wisconsin Sociologist*, *8*(Spring):3-19, 1971.

Raine, W. "The Perception of Police Brutality in South Central Los Angeles," in N. Cohen (Ed.): *The Los Angeles Riot*. New York: Praeger, 1970, pp. 380-412.

Rosenbaum, R. J. "Los Gorras Blancas of San Miguel County, 1889-1890," in R. Rosaldo et al. (Eds.): *Chicano: The Evolution of a People*. Minneapolis: Winston, 1973, pp. 128-133.

Schlesinger, A. B. Los Gorras Blancas, 1889-1891. *J of Mexican American History*, *1*(Spring):87-143, 1971.

Sleepy Lagoon Defense Committee. *The Sleepy Lagoon Case*. Los Angeles: Citizens' Committee for the Defense of Mexican-American Youth, 1942.

Smith, P. E., and Hawkins, R. O. Victimization, types of citizen-police contacts, and attitudes toward the police. *Law and Society Rev*, *8*(Fall):135-152, 1973.

Trujillo, L. D. La Evolution del Bandido 'al Pachuco': a critical examination and evaluation of criminological literature on Chicanos. *Issues in Criminology*, *9*(Fall):43-67, 1974.

U. S. Bureau of the Census. *Persons of Spanish Origin in the United States: March 1976.* Current Population Reports. Series P-20, No. 302. Washington, D.C.: U. S. Government Printing Office, 1976.

U. S. Commission of Civil Rights. *Mexican Americans and the Administration of Justice in the Southwest.* Washington, D.C.: U.S. Government Printing Office, 1970, p. iii.

Webb, W. P. *The Texas Ranger.* Austin: University of Texas Press, 1965.

Webb. W. P. *The Texas Rangers in the Mexican War.* Austin: Jenkins Garrett Press, 1975.

Section III

THEORETICAL IMPLICATIONS

CHAPTER 7

ON THE STRUCTURE OF ETHNIC CRIME IN AMERICA: THE MODERN FORM OF BUCCANEER CAPITALISM

KENNETH L. AND W. ALLEN MARTIN

IT IS NO LONGER true that capital is the preeminent ingredient for success in modern industrial society. This fact is of vital importance for understanding the nature and goals of ethnic crime during the latter part of this century. Only recently have students of ethnic crime shed traditional sociological explanations of ethnic crime as resulting from anomie (Humphries, 1973) or structural disadvantage (Cloward and Ohlin, 1960; Merton, 1957), and moved to a more fertile line of thought: much of crime, today, is operated in the manner of business enterprise (Sparks, 1979; Light, 1977a; Ianni, 1972; 1974; Haller, 1970; Bell, 1960; 1963; Smith, 1981, 1982). Though promising, this line of inquiry is often hindered by an implicit assumption that capital is still the *sine qua non*. There is another equally important ingredient in the success equation of modern America—monopolistic business structure (O'Connor, 1974; Galbraith, 1971; Averitt, 1968). The major payoff of ethnic crime in the latter part of this century has been the generation of both capital and market control (in the form of oligopolies and monopolies). This particular form of structure not only ensures the retention and stabilization of wealth generated through crime but, in addition, allows the criminal organization to become more legitimate by changing to legitimate suppliers, buyers, and even products and services, thereby achieving propriety.

For our analysis, it is useful to divide the history of the American economy into two phases: early capitalism and modern corporatism.

Early capitalism was dominated by more open markets and more by entrepreneurs and small companies. Modern corporatism is dominated by imperfect competition — oligopolies and monopolies — and by corporate giants (Dewey, 1969; Martin, 1981; for documentation, see Parenti, 1983:11-15).

Crime has been used as a stepping stone to wealth and status throughout both phases via the classic process of "buccaneer capitalism" first identified by Pirenne (1913). Many authors since Pirenne have studied this avenue to wealth.

These investigators have overlooked the point that forms the main thesis of this paper: the development of large criminal organizations coincides with the onset of modern corporatism. During imperfect competition capital loses preeminance, while market control through oligopolies and monopolies becomes the *sine qua non*. Thus, the form of "buccaneer capitalism" itself has changed with the new economy. Whereas the use of large volumes of capital may have been sufficient to grant legitimacy during perfect competition, today it is the organizational structure which helps to provide legitimacy and stabilized wealth.

Following is a brief analysis of crime in early capitalism covering a period roughly between the thirteenth and the seventeenth centuries. A more detailed argument is then presented on the need of enterprises (illegal and otherwise) to form organizations under modern corporatism. In the "Conclusions" section it is pointed out that another important difference between the two periods is the timing of racial and ethnic minorities' participation in the process of buccaneer capitalism. Their participation did not begin until the second, most recent phase which suggests certain implications for majority-minority group relations.

Crime During the Rise and Development of Early Capitalism

The use of illegal activities to gain capital had its origins in the early development of capitalism and thus can be traced to the leading capitalistic countries of the world, Northern Europe and the United States. It was a common means to success utilized by the core English culture and other Northern European groups which eventually blended into what is now recognized as the "majority" in the United States.

Pirenne (1913) and Sombart (1915) were probably the first to recognize the significance of this process. Pirenne sketched cases of individuals' rise to the capitalist class in England during the thirteenth century, and uncovers a key sequence: enterprising individuals from poor backgrounds were able to ascend to the capitalist class by engaging in marginally illicit enterprise or in other types of business activity that the upper class considered questionable. When these individuals had gained enough capital, they invested it in land and the purchase of titles, abandoning their less-legitimate business pursuits.

Sombart extended this sketch to the following centuries of European expansion and colonialism. He argued that piracy became a way of life with astounding proportions. In the sixteenth and seventeenth centuries, there were at least 400 pirate vessels operating in the English Channel (Sombart, 1915:68). In America, along the coast of the Carolinas, more that 1,500 pirates operated (1915:69). Almost every colony had some connection with sea robbery. Sombart made a convincing case for the fact that much of the financial support for capitalism, developing during this time period, derived from outright freebooting and privateering. Many, if not most, of these pirates were eventually able to convert their operations into more legitimate concerns and became respectable noblemen.

Many noblemen became freebooters to bolster their waning estates. This group included such names as Sir Walter Raleigh, Sir Francis Drake, Sir Martin Frobisher, and Sir Richard Greenville (Sombart, 1915:71). The intimate connection between crime and capitalism has not been lost on radical theorists (Eitzen and Timmer, 1985), and the putative moral dilemmas posed by the criminals' route to capitalistic success were important to Spencer's philosophy (see especially 1884: 107-148). More recently, Andrews (1966) conducted a sophisticated historical analysis of privateering during the Elizabethan period, 1585 to 1603. He details the connections between privateering, piracy, international trade relations, and the deterioration of British relations with Spain and France.

Veblen took this argument further in his classic work on the leisure class (1899, especially pp. 117-118). Veblen claimed that wealth (or property) was such a powerful factor as a legitimizer of status that it cut across, and indeed canceled, all other claims to legitimation — including behaving in a "law-abiding" manner. Veblen argued that even theft of property would directly convey prestige **provided that the theft was large enough**, and that it was pursued for status-enhancing purposes. Some would argue that before the turn of the past century, the direct control of capital was instantaneously legitimizing in the eye of the general public, regardless of the legal or illegal nature of its mode of acquisition.

Crime in Modern Corporatism

In the past few decades of the twentieth century, we have witnessed the growth of the multi-plant firm resulting eventually in oligopolies and monopolies—dominating the national economy (Averitt, 1968; Dewey, 1969; Galbraith, 1971). In this kind of economy, most great wealth is organizationally based, and thus, simple property-holding (Veblen's principle) is no longer sufficient to make a life of crime "respectable" and "legitimate." Following is a description of some of the essential characteristics of oligopolistic and monopolistic firms. As noted above, these firms, in the aggregate, compose the most central and powerful sector of our economy, and they serve as the logical model for less-legitimate organizations which aspire to great profitability and eventual respectability.

Large Scale Organization: The Model for Organized Crime. Galbraith (1971) argues that large firms have turned the tables on consumers. Whereas these firms were once controlled by consumers through the market, now these firms control consumers and hence demand. They are able to accomplish control of consumers through their size which, of itself, creates market domination and monopoly "pools" in their surrounding geographical areas. Also, the aim of corporate advertising most recently has been to create "wants" and to "push" consumers to buy their products rather than to inform. But most important of all is that firms of this type tend toward vertical integration (Averitt, 1968). That is, they often establish control over sources of supply and of consumer outlets.

The second feature of large firms is their ability to maintain internal cash reserves. This feature insulates the firm from government tampering with their long-run investment goals. The government may attempt to regulate investments, in the interests of the national economy, by raising or lowering interest rates for borrowing. Large firms can pursue investments in accordance with their own goals and needs so long as they can "borrow from themselves."

Third, large firms can finance influence at both the local and national levels of government. Governmental influence is especially important to the large firm, in part because governmental policy, especially foreign policy, can have significant effects on both short-run profits and long-run planning.

There are other important features of large-scale firms, but for the purposes of the following analysis, let's concentrate on these three.

Organization of Illegitimate Enterprise. On all three counts, less-legitimate organizations appear to resemble the corporate model. Furthermore, an illegal market appears to present especially fertile ground for the development of a monopolistic domination of markets.

The first feature of large-scale business enterprise is the control of demand through the control of the consumer: this is one of the most important and consciously developed features of organized crime. Previously, the economic model has been limited to "demand-oriented" crime and excluded "predatory" crime (most recently, see Light, 1977a; Smith, 1975), even though it is understood that a criminal organization may participate in both types of crime (Abadinsky, 1983, persuasively argues that this relationship is common). This distinction derives primarily from an attempt to use the classical microeconomic theory of perfect competition as the model for criminal business organization. This theory clearly does not provide for the types of influence processes that predatory crime may entail.

Predatory crime is more understandable from this first feature of the corporate model. The larger-scale organization can gain greater control over market processes and control over the supply of raw materials and commodities for sale in the market. With this model, predatory crime differs from demand-oriented crime primarily in the strength and directness of the influence process. This proposition follows from the key point of this section of the paper. More-legitimate enterprise in an imperfect-competition economy differs from less-legitimate enterprise, mainly in the strength and directness of the influence process. The three forms of activity—legitimate imperfect competition, demand-oriented crime, and predatory crime—fall on a continuum of influence proceeding from the least to the strongest and with the most direct influence. (See Sparks, 1979, for a general definition of what he calls "crime as business" which includes some activities which others have labeled "predatory crime.") Legitimate perfect competition forms the zero-point on the influence scale.

Protection is often sold to retailers by giving the retailers something to be protected from. There are dope "pushers" as well as dope "dealers." Prostitutes and pimps engage in "hustling" as well as "providing." Gambling, among the most "demand-oriented" of crimes, produces built-in ties between the "sellers" and the "consumers." Systems for catching

"suckers" are well-known in the betting world. Easy wins early in the relationship, coupled with intermittent wins is one of the surest ways that
an operator can establish control over a gambler. But, perhaps the best
system ever devised for gaining control over gamblers is numbers gambling. The bettor selects a number between 000 and 999 but only gets
paid off in the odds of around 600 to 1. Thus, small bets reap infre-
quent, but large returns (which from an operant conditioning point of
view is ideal for generating control of the subject), and the operator
makes a profit of four hundred dollars on every thousand dollars bet.

Beyond these types of incentives, the criminal operator has other
built-in protections for exorbitant pricing strategies. He may point to
the risk he is taking, since "after all it is illegal." He may cloak himself
with the fear generated by the criminal organization he represents to
prevent questions about odds or the price of drugs. Finally, the very illegality of the service adds to the control of the operating organization
over the consumer, since the police act to reduce the alternatives available to the consumer. If he wants the service, he has to pay the price.

There is a great (and apparently inelastic) demand for illegal services. Light's (1977b) analysis of the functionality of numbers gambling
for the consumer is quite compelling in this regard. Nevertheless, it is
important to recognize that much of the demand for services or products
can be generated by the oligopolistic or monopolistic firm (Galbraith,
1971), and the prices of these services and products can be predeter-
mined by the firm to a point where profits are maximal. If these services
or products are illegal, their illegality adds to the mechanisms available
to the criminal organization for generating demand and fixing prices.
As a result, consumer interest can be bound to the criminal organization
for longer periods of time, thus ensuring a stable market, and the range
for price fixing is greater, thus ensuring especially large profits.

At first, a less-legitimate enterprise probably resorts more often to
raw force to gain control over consumers, depending on the type of
crime in question. But, over time, criminal managers learn that less-
problematic control can be maintained through vertical integration.
Once control of supply sources is established (monopsony) and the consumer market is cornered (monopoly), the less-legitimate organization
can relax its cruder strategies of direct control. The second feature of
large-scale organization—the ability to maintain cash reserves—is necessary for the growth of more-legitimate and less-legitimate organizations. Funds for investment from legal sources are more problematic for

enterprises toward the illegal end of the continuum. For example, they may be less able to tap legitimate credit markets. But in addition to this negative inducement, there is a positive inducement to maintain cash reserves that are not available to more legitimate corporations. The organization can operate as a bank for loansharking. Money can be loaned to people who cannot establish credit at usurious rates. Sometimes "enforcers" are used to pressure people who fall behind in their payments, but most often "enforcers" are not used nor are they necessary. If the individual does not pay his debt, then he will lose his only source of money since he cannot get legitimate credit (Ianni, 1974).

As the criminal organization grows and expands its business interests in various directions, governmental influence, the third feature of large-scale organization, is necessary. Governmental connections serve in part to keep the organization abreast of new directions in governmental policy which may affect the organization's business. But these connections can also provide influence. Ianni (1972) presents a detailed case history of an Italian crime organization where two of its members have developed extensive contacts in the local and national governments. These members act as any other lobbyists providing elaborate gifts and entertainment to politicians. In addition to the organization's interest in pending legislation, these members deal effectively with problems from federal regulatory bodies through their political contacts.

In summary with both predatory and less-predatory crime, large-scale, especially monopolistic, business organization is the ideal. The fact that the businesses are illegal only serves to strengthen their control over their customers: the more illegally emeshed the customers become, the more they can be controlled. Law enforcement serves to reduce competition, and the ever-present possibility of violence serves to firm up the vertical integration of the organization through its supply sources and consumer outlets in addition to, at times, aiding in the control of recalcitrant consumers.

The Move to Legitimization. "Buccaneers" eventually abandon less-legitimate activities once they have sufficient resources to maintain stable wealth and respectability in a more-legitimate activity. The necessary resources for legitimization in the modern corporate economy are both capital and large-scale business organization. A strong and elaborate less-legitimate organization possesses a requisite for profitable survival in legitimate business activity.

With only capital, it is not as likely that a less-legitimate entrepreneur will find legitimate growth opportunities within a modern corporate society. Averitt (1968) points out that much of our economy still operates on the economic principles of early capitalism, where perfect competition is the rule; this is the "periphery economy." One option open to the criminal is to amass capital through illegal activities which can then be invested in more-legitimate business in the periphery economy. But the periphery economy is where the smallest yet most numerous businesses are found. Since this sector is in perfect competition, the lives of businesses in the periphery are often short, profits depending strictly on the market and the whims of the consumers. (See Garrity, 1968, for the problems confronting "black capitalism" when it is operated on a small scale.)

The "center economy" is where most of our industrial strength is found (Averitt, 1968). But the entrepreneur, whether more or less legitimate, cannot enter this sector alone with only capital in hand. The center economy is dominated by oligopolies and corporate giants. Only the large-scale criminal organization is a serious contender for entry into the center economy. The criminal organization may enter the center economy by moving gradually into more-legitimate business or more-legitimate business methods while retaining its organizational interlinkages among the individual businesses it has acquired.

Thus, the process of buccaneer capitalism, in an imperfect-competition economy, is completed through the formation of a legitimate corporate conglomerate. In early capitalism, a sufficient goal of the process was to acquire capital which would be invested by a single individual. Today, such individual initiative is most likely to result in confinement in the "periphery economy." Corporate organization provides the surest and most enduring avenue to success in modern America.

Examples of illegitimate minority organizations that eventually became legitimate seem to begin with the Irish. (See Bell, 1963 and 1960, on this point and the other examples which follow.) Some organized to control the waterfront in New York, in addition to construction and trucking, through a system of directors. The power garnered from these areas was eventually trained on local and statewide political machinery. The Irish came to be heavily represented on the police force; legitimacy and respectability soon followed.

As the Irish organizations moved toward more legitimate enterprise, they were replaced by some Jewish organizations. It is best to distinguish between those of the earlier German Jewish immigrants and the later East European Jewish organizations (Sklare, 1971). The German Jews were initially the most successful minority group, often succeeding as merchants or investment bankers. It was the Eastern European Jews who were trapped in ghettos, particularly in New York. Some of these Jews, though, found the convenient ladder to success through organized crime as described by Bell. The names of Arnold Rothstein, Lepke Buchalter, and Gurrah Shapiro became infamous as industrial racketeers and gambling operators. The less-legitimate organizations were soon abandoned for more legitimate concerns.

In the late thirties, southern Italians began to take over organized crime as the Eastern European Jews moved into legitimate business. The mass media have played up the case of Italians as forming a unique national syndicate which has been in the business of subverting national interests in the pursuit of huge profits. But from all indications (Bell, 1963; Ianni, 1972), illegitimate Italian organizations were similar in form and intent to those of the Irish and the Jews. Far from forming the national superorganization that it had been reputed to possess, Italian less-legitimate enterprises, like their two predecessors, have been gradually shifting to more-legitimate enterprises and methods. For example, Ianni (1972) details the history of one Italian "family's" rise in crime and gradual movement into the legitimate center economy with organization intact. He also presents compelling case studies of the Black, Puerto Rican, and Cuban groups (1974) which suggest that these organizations are establishing more-legitimate enterprises in the center economy.

The process of buccaneer capitalism reveals a unique path of mobility for minorities. The less-legitimate organization, which eventually becomes legitimate, offers primary employment not only to individual minority members, but it provides for the mobility of whole businesses from the competitive "periphery economy" to the sheltered "center economy." Potentially, such organizations can move the major part of an ethnic enclave into the prosperous center economy.

Historically, large business organizations have been the domain of only the majority. And these large enterprises have grown in part from their exploitation of unprotected minorities. In the case of crime and the growth of ethnic oligopolies and monopolies through crime, there has been a unique reversal of this historical precedent. Just as large legitimate business organizations have been able to turn the tables on consumers, less-legitimate organizations have been able to turn the tables of majority-minority exploitation. The less-legitimate organization may grow and prosper and break the flow of funds which is overbalanced in favor of the majority. It can do this by exploiting majority members in addition to its own ethnic community.

Ianni (1974) describes a black businessman who is part of a newly forming black criminal organization in Harlem. Besides loansharking, an activity directed mostly toward members of his community, he also engages in the buying and selling of stolen goods. In clothes, for example, he deals mostly in goods stolen from an exclusive group of men's stores "downtown" (the term he uses to refer to the rich, majority-owned, clothiers in New York). He sells these clothes to other blacks in Harlem at a 40 percent discount. He makes money and the blacks in Harlem, the ones willing to buy stolen property, can get quality goods that they could not normally afford. In another example, Light (1977b) points out that black numbers running is no longer directed exclusively toward blacks; most of the numbers gamblers are not black.

Both processes, the criminal organizations' exploitation of its own community and the exploitation of majority members, serve to halt the outflow of cash reserves from the minority community and even to reverse the flow, bringing in more money to the community to counterbalance the money that escapes the community. As the organization grows, it provides an important source of new jobs for ethnic members and the community as a whole prospers.

CONCLUSIONS

The ultimate goal of ethnic-based crime today is the same as that of the buccaneer capitalists of earlier centuries: legitimization into the upper strata. Today's minorities, however, must establish large-scale organizations if they are to maximize their upward mobility. Now, in an era of imperfect competition, high position in a large-scale organization is both a sign of and the means to elite status. Since it is apparently easier to begin in less-legitimate business than in more-legitimate business, some minority members reasonably seek the easier route. Thus, law enforcement has a deeply rooted problem. The problem is exacerbated by the realization that less-legitimate minority enterprise is positioned along a continuum which nears and even includes respectable enterprises. And the propriety of today's less-legitimate minority enterprises is no worse than the early buccaneer capitalist, many of whom achieved the apex of respectability.

Progress against less-legitimate minority enterprise cannot be achieved without an improved understanding of the continuum of enterprise legitimacy. We must begin with the history of more- and less-legitimate enterprise and then study today's requisites for successful enterprise and upward social mobility. Then we must provide a structure by which minorities can compete in more-legitimate enterprises.

REFERENCES

Abadinsky, H. Professional and Organized Crime: A Symbiosis. Paper presented at the Academy of Criminal Justice Sciences Annual Meeting in San Antonio, Texas (March), 1983.

Andrews, K. R. *Elizabethan Privateering*. Cambridge: Cambridge University Press, 1966.

Averitt, R. T. *The Dual Economy: The Dynamics of American Industry Structure*. New York: Norton and Company, Inc., 1968.

Bell, D. *The End of Ideology*. Rev. Ed. New York: Free Press, 1960.

Bell, D. The myth of the Cosa Nostra. *The New Leader*, (December):12-15, 1963.

Cloward, R., and Lloyd E. O. *Delinquency and Opportunity*. Glencoe: Free Press, 1960.

Cressey, D. R. *Criminal Organization: Its Elementary Forms*. New York: Harper and Row, 1972.

Dewey, D. *The Theory of Imperfect Competition: A Radical Reconstruction*. New York: Columbia University Press, 1969.

Galbraith, J. K. *The New Industrial State*. New York: Mentor, 1971.

Garrity, J. T. Red ink for ghetto industries. *Harvard Business Review*, (June/July), 1968.

Gordon, D. M. *Theories of Poverty and Underemployment: Orthodox, Radical, and Dual Labor Market Perspectives*. Massachusetts: Lexington Books, 1972.

Haller, M. H. Urban crime and criminal justice: the Chicago case. *Journal of American History*, *57*:618-35, 1970.

Harrison, B. *Education, Training, and the Urban Ghetto*. Baltimore: The Johns Hopkins University Press, 1972.

Humphries, R. A. L. Crime and criminology. *Encyclopedia Americana*, *8*:193-201, 1973.

Ianni, F. A. J. *A Family Business: Kinship and Social Control in Organized Crime*. New York: Russell Sage, 1972.

Ianni, F. A. J. *Black Mafia: Ethnic Succession in Organized Crime*. New York: Simon and Schuster, 1974, pp. 37-47.

Light, I. The ethnic vice industry, 1880-1944. *American Sociological Review*, *42*(June):464-479, 1977a.

Light, I. Numbers gambling. *American Sociological Review*, *42*(December):892-904, 1977b.

Martin, W. A. Toward specifying a spectrum-based theory of enterprise. *Criminal Justice Review*, *6*(Spring):54-57, 1981.

Merton, R. K. *Social Theory and Social Structure*. Rev. Ed. New York: Free Press, 1957.

O'Connor, J. *The Fiscal Crisis of the State*. New York: St. Martin's Press, 1973.

Pirenne, H. The states in the social history of capitalism. *Social Science Reprints*, 1913.

Smith, D. C., Jr. Organized crime and entrepreneurship. *International Journal of Criminology and Penology*, *6*:161-177, 1978.

Smith, D. C., Jr. Paragons, pariahs, and pirates: a spectrum-based theory of enterprise. *Crime and delinquency*, *26*:358-386, 1980.

CHAPTER 8

SURVIVORS AND CONNIVERS: THE ADAPTATION OF EXTRA-LEGAL BEHAVIOR BY NEW RUSSIAN IMMIGRANTS

LYDIA S. ROSNER

THERE HAS always been a close association between the immigrant and the rise of American sociology. For it was just as the
largest wave of immigration hit our shores, between the years of 1890-
1924, that a new discipline reached out to make this new tide the object
of its study. Sociology minutely examined the immigrant and became
engrossed with the issues and social problems inherent in the urbanization, ghettoization and acculturation of this new population. Crime, culture and ethnic boundaries were examined by a discipline involved in
attempting to solve social problems, and theoretical and scholarly works
of sociologists reflected a nation absorbed in the absorption of a new and
different population.

Those new immigrants were far different, both in appearance and in
culture, from the Northern European forefathers who had settled
America. The immigrants upon whom sociology looked, those who
flooded these shores during those turn-of-the-century years, came from
the lands of Southern and Eastern Europe—Italy, Greece, Austria-
Hungary, Serbia, Rumania, Russian Poland and Russia—"the tired,
the poor, the huddled masses yearning to breathe free" about whom
Emma Lazarus wrote. Their problems and their transitions provided
American-Protestant society and sociology, in particular, with an en-
grossing subject matter.

103

From the study of this population were built theories of crime and criminality; and, indeed, a review of the literature in the field of American criminology demonstrates that culture-conflicts, marginality, and deviant behavior, fostered by often unattainable goals of success, all reflect the immigrant experience somewhere within their theoretical perspectives. Suggested in this literature is the concept that the new immigrant, a peasant or villager, arriving from a peasant society, unable to move into the mainstreams of American society in acceptable fashion, satisfied his desires for success through extra-legal means.

Daniel Bell (1953) has suggested that this immigrant used crime as a way of climbing the "queer ladder of social mobility" which he defines as peculiarly American. And Francis Ianni (1974) offers the prospect of ethnic succession, of one immigrant group succeeding another and providing those services which members of society are willing to pay for even though illegal. This prospect of group after group taking over the reins as providers of illegal service is postulated by sociologists and criminologists. In part, this concept sees the immigrant as an "outsider," one who cannot and does not understand the society into which he has come, because his was a less complex, often peasant society and thus supplied him with little of value with which to enter mainstream American life.

It is time to reexamine sociology's attachment to the immigrant which produced theories of his criminality. These theories were based upon problems inherent in the industrialization, ghettoization, detribalization of the peasant and his entry into this industrialized society with marginal skills and which left him and his children with a myriad of social-psychological problems, in turn producing anomic behavior and crime. Theoretically, we are without an explanation of the criminality of the immigrant who arrives on these shores with applicable social, urban and industrial skills; without a body of work which documents how the immigrant who arrives with those industrial and social skills needed to enter our society translates these skills upon immigration.

In part, the absence of this body of work is due to the absence of immigrants. The heavy influx of immigrants in the early twentieth century was curbed by the passage of the Johnson Immigration Act of 1924. Those who had immigrated from the Southern European countries have had a chance to produce, on these shores, second and third generations of Americans. And success ladders have been established for both those who moved through criminal and those who moved through legal channels in order to enter the mainstream. The university and the workplace urbanized even those whose ancestors came from the most peasant of beginnings. The huddled masses and their decendants were no longer visible.

But, starting in 1965, as a result of changes in the U.S. immigration laws, a new type of immigrant arrived upon the American shores. Unlike the early immigrants who came from a society which had hardly prepared them for the life in industrialized America, these new immigrants had experienced varying degrees of industrialization, urbanization and modern bureaucracy. The shtetl, the potato field, the small peasant village are not of his point of origin. As the United States has industrialized, so has the world. And even those who have had few dealings with technologies in their home countries are aware, because of the advent of world wide communication, that a technology exists and is within reach. Many of these new immigrants are schooled in the workings of modern industrial materials and have skills that are applicable in the open marketplace. This new immigrant thus arrives into a society which, in some fashion, parallels the one from which he came, and he brings with him understandings of technology which are the results of a degree of urbanization and industrialization in his home country. Additionally (and of particular interest to sociologists and criminologists), this new immigrant has had experience in dealing with bureaucracy. His experience in third-world and socialist countries have given him skills and abilities in dealing with bureaucracy that often equal, and in some instances surpass, his American counterparts.

Through this new immigrant we see that crime has become qualitatively different. What was seen in the literature as white-collar crime, crime of the rich, crime of big business, crime of those who had access to systems and the currency of those systems is, in fact, the crime of anyone with access to a bureaucratic system. And the immigrant from a society where bureaucracy is already the characteristic institution of his world comes to these shores equipped to participate and often lead in the manipulation of the systems of the very new land into which he has immigrated though he has to learn the particulars of the new forms of American social welfare and other bureaucracies.

The Immigrant from the U.S.S.R.

I have examined a population of new immigrants who have arrived from the Soviet Union since the early 1970s. They are indeed a product of the ultimate bureaucracy—one which governs every aspect of their lives through every waking and sleeping minute. Examining their adaptive behavior both within their homeland and within their new land has provided specific insights into new areas of crime which command attention.

This new immigrant from the Soviet Union is one who has lived within a totally bureaucratic system; he has had to rely on the government for access to all goods and services. Those goods and services that were not often within his reach, due to shortages in production and failures in distribution, became available through a vast amount of corruption and criminality in which all within that system partake in some way or another. These immigrants, in my interviews, reveal that they have the most intimate contact with such corruption. This is not to say that there are not other immigrants, from other countries, who arrive on these shores schooled in a variety of manipulations and circumventions of legality. However, my research was limited to those who have come from the Soviet Union and who are blue collar or skilled workers. I have not looked at the intellectual, because: (1) they fell outside my sample area (Brighton Beach), (2) they have traditionally been outside the normal system of production and distribution: and (3) they are involved in a different variety of immigration problems. Thus, the dissidents and protestors are not part of this study.

The population studied can be classified as either survivors or connivers. The survivor (necessary criminal), while in the Sovet Union, elected to beat the system in order to live with a system that had limited access to goods and services. This behavior within the U.S.S.R. was the usual behavior of the average citizen. Beating the system provided them with minimal standards of goods, services, and comforts. Within the United States, survivors do those things which provide comfort to their families and which allow them to move rapidly into mainstream American society. In some instances, this may mean illegal activity, in that they collect welfare while working, that they qualify for welfare and food stamps by concealing income, or that they use Medicaid services for which they are not eligible. The new Russian is able to do this, because he has had long practice before his immigration with the kinds of illegal paper manipulation or circumvention of governmental regulation which gains them entitlement services.

The conniver within the Soviet Union elected to use the system in order to profit substantially. He was concerned not only with just surviving, but with enjoying the good life through criminal activity. He had to learn how to profit within an illegal, repressive system while illegally manipulating goods and services for personal or professional gain. Already skilled in beating the system and indeed with profiting from this system beating, the conniver, upon immigration, enters a world of criminality which becomes available for him because of his earlier achieved skill in these same areas and his prior commitment and association with the criminal world in achieving his livelihood within his homeland. For him, the new bureaucracy is an easy one to circumvent. These new immigrants identify for us several areas of criminality in a technological and industrialized world.

Three particular aspects of this crime are to be discussed here. The first involves **paper manipulation** — a kind of crime which demonstrates how extra legal behavior can be imported together with the immigrant. The second and third, **nationalization** and **internationalization** of crime, serve to demonstrate how skills already honed in a repressive bureaucratic society can flourish when allowed access to a multi-jurisdictional and less-repressive new climate.

Paper Manipulation

For the average American citizen, papers are not of central importance: a driver's license, a birth certificate, a social security card are viewed as replaceable documents. Put your license renewal application into the assigned box, sit down and wait, and expect to be called. Such is the average American's understanding of what happens to papers. If for some reason you are not called within an expected time period, then you blame, out loud if possible, the sloppiness of the motor vehicle bureau, the lazy and uninterested behavior of the clerk who while chewing gum discussed her last live-in roommate, or the ineptitude of the bureaucracy who assigned too few people to shephard such a long line. At worst, you assume that someone misplaced the papers and resolution can be accomplished, same day, same office. Never does it occur to the average American that either the waiting time or the lack of prompt resolution is an attack on his very existence, some bureaucratic agenda of those in power meant to deny you, your specific existence, your papers — for a specific public or private reason.

The clerk within the bureau, too, assumes that papers left in a basket will be deposited by the person in whose name the papers are to be completed. When calling up a name from the line, the clerk expects and assumes that the person responding will be the person who placed the papers in the basket in the first place. The clerks expectations allow for manipulation by those who have the skills to circumvent the system. For American papers are but a by-product of the specific administrative need for car identification, tax identification, or travel identification. A person does not need certification of his identity in this country, except for such purposes.

It is difficult for the new Russian immigrants to understand that a person does not need personal identification papers. For a citizen of the Soviet Union, papers **are** the person. In some instances, they are more real than the person. While in the Soviet Union, they had to have the right paper, the approved paper or the revised paper. Russians who immigrate have to have proper papers in order to exit the Soviet Union. They also must have proper papers in order to enter this country. Therefore, even among those who do not engage in major criminal acts, there are certain understandings which acknowledge these needs and activities in regard to the use of papers.

Having grown up with a respect for and fear of loss of bureaucratic papers, even those who do not engage in major criminality have arrived in the U.S. with the ability to circumvent bureaucratic dealings through the paid intervention of people who produce the desired results without resorting to bureaucratic agency personnel. Prior immigrants from the earlier immigrations have borrowed papers for entry, switched passports and such; but the growth of bureaucracy in this country and the bureaucratic nature of the home country of recent Russian immigrants has created fertile soil for a major enterprise in paper manipulation.

Thus, this new immigration has brought to these shores those who have made a living within the Soviet Union doing forgery and reproduction. They have continued to make their living here doing the same. Even those who later move on to the world of the legitimate citizen have often begun with purchase of illegal papers. The academic degree which is reproduced here for job reference, the driver's license which is reproduced to be shown at the motor vehicle bureau as proof of driving skill (and immediate access to a New York license without a test), are the lesser criminal areas of paper manipulation.

Paper manipulation reaches throughout the new Russian immigrant community. There is a buyer, a maker, and a seller of forged paper. There is the person who needs work and has to get a driver's license so that he can move on to a legitimate activity, and there is a person who forges passports, green cards and credit cards. For some, the making of papers was a professional activity worthy of respect within the Soviet Union. For others, the purchase of papers serves only to affirm a necessity: the way to help parents exit the U.S.S.R., and perhaps the way to reach optimum employment possibilities within the United States.

For others still, this kind of paper manipulation extends the kind of criminal opportunities which were not ever viewed a part of immigrant crime. Not only can documents be supplied to the internal immigrant community, whether it be Russian or not, but documents can be forged which opens the world to other major kinds of criminality.

For this new Russian immigrant, the conniver, skilled in the making of paper, has entered a world which is in the process of becoming a paper economy. Credit cards take the place of currency, bank transfers take the place of personal transactions. Paper manipulation takes on even more importance in the new world of this immigrant, for he is involved with the endless possibilities of a growing field—one which can take him far beyond the making of personal or governmental documents. The ability to make paper can be translated into national and international travel through the making of tickets and necessary travel documents, into major financial activity through currency forgery for national and international purposes and through stock and bond forgery.

Additionally, though outside the area of paper manipulation, this new immigrant conniver already understands these markets for papers and is skilled in counterfeiting. He involves himself in the counterfeiting of antiques and icons worth millions of dollars and in demand by collectors world-wide. The learnings acquired through a lifetime of deviant behavior in the home country are adapted immediately upon immigration. Insurance scams, the ability to create money through legal and illegal means, the entry into markets for symbols rather than things, imply a sophistication in criminality far beyond that which has previously been regarded as applicable to immigrant crime. For these criminals, already of middle-class orientation, entering the sophisticated world of American business through the purchase of stores and galleries, the "queer ladder of social mobility" seems to already have been climbed, previous to immigration. In fact, their ability to live well, to travel, to eat and drink the fruits of their harvest, is only extended upon immigration.

Unlike their predecessors in immigrant crime, this new immigrant, comes with extra-legal behavior patterns which allow him access to a system where such patterns are less needed. In fact, skilled in bureaucratic maneuvering in a system which operates 24 hours a day, he finds relative ease in continuing criminality in a less rigid system, without constant surveillance, and where the expectations of the bureaucracy do not allow for his sophistication in crime.

Nationalization of Crime

Studies of previous immigrations focused on the culture of the slum and the ghetto and in some way made association between the culture of poverty that exists in these places and a life of crime. At the same time that sociologists of the day were studying the immigrant, they were also trying to understand the kinds of crime that either exists or originates in areas of social disorganization. And the ghetto looked socially disorganized to the American reformers and sociologists who viewed as foreign and unappealing those lower-class immigrants who peopled those crowded urban streets of their cities. To study the immigrant and the ghettos, one did not have to go far from the great universities. Just across town there often (and conveniently) existed a learning laboratory. Immigrant crime was localized, just where it could easily be studied — localized and identifiable, and viewed as having its origins in these urban ghettos.

With the industrialization of society and the advent of a new technology, the world is smaller. Transportation and communications networks have allowed nationalization and internationalization of relationships. Relatives who have immigrated to one country have the opportunity to talk with and often to visit relatives who have immigrated to another. And criminal skills and activities often originate prior to immigration rather than in the ghettoes created by new, more sophisticated immigrants.

Within the Soviet Union, one cannot travel without proper identification. One cannot visit a relative in another city without proper papers. Travel is restricted and movement for illegal purposes involves manipulation of documents and of personnel in order to enter a city and to remain there illegally. One cannot even move ones residence from one city to another within the Soviet Union without proper documentation proving reassignment to that city by the government for work purposes. Yet, there are those who have learned how to travel illegally within the Soviet Union, and there the airplane is a major vehicle for grey market and black market operation. Upon immigration, they discover that movement within the United States is unrestricted. In fact, they discover that movement within the world is virtually unrestricted.

With the ability to manipulate the bureaucracy within the Soviet Union and without being hampered by governmental surveillance, the conniver is able to take his illegal dealings on tour. Because local police departments in American cities have jurisdictional constraints, it is only becoming evident that among these new immigrants, crimes, which have previously been considered of a local nature, have become national.

This population has, as one New York City Police Department Intelligence Division, Organized Crime Monitoring Unit Detective puts it, "learned to maneuver on our airlines and on our turnpikes." He describes how someone will fly to Cincinatti, go into a large department store, emerge with furs and other stolen items and then fly them to New York to fence them. Law enforcement sources, both national and international, are confirming to each other the fact that an unusual number of Russian emigrants are involved in felony charges within a multiplicity of jurisdictions.

What has been considered local crime has taken on a national and international flavor because of previous experience of the new immigrant. Within the Soviet Union, one would pick farm produce in one area of the country and carry that produce to an airplane, fly the produce to a northern city and personally sell that produce on a street corner. The ability and understandings involved in that kind of small-scale activity has now taken on larger proportions. Bureaucratic restraints within the Soviet Union were often circumvented. Lack of such restraints here in the United States of America allows those so inclined to expand, even the most common of criminal pursuits, into multi-jurisdictional areas. At present, police departments in major American cities are attempting to develop networks of communication that will allow them to identify those who are engaged in such activities.

Specifically different, too, is the scope of criminal activities involved in by any one conniver. Unlike the literature which sees a *modus operandi*, a crime characteristic or a particular person, this population dabbles in different illegal activities at the same time. The same person who might be involved in jewelry scams in Philadelphia might be involved in a burglary in New York or forgery in Los Angeles. Travel throughout the nation and involvement in different kinds of illegal activities by the same individual makes this criminal difficult to identify. Paper manipulation and false documentation which are part of the connivers inventory of criminal skills makes apprehension even harder.

Internalization of Crime

This conniver population, but a small part of those new immigrants to this country, is different from large segments of criminal populations studied by earlier sociologists and criminologists. The ability to commit crime in one city, state, or nation and then move on to another city, state, or nation is unique in the history of immigrant crime. Mobility, facilitated by cheap and easy access to transportation, without complicated proof of status, allows this population to enlarge their territory in a way that was not charted among criminals before.

The FBI, Customs, Immigration as well as various international law enforcement agencies are forced to investigate world-wide crimes such as drug trafficking, jewel theft and monetary manipulations, all of which have involved new immigrants. This changing pattern of international criminality reflects the changes in communication and transportation in an ever-shrinking world.

With the ability to manipulate paper, that is, to gain access to international travel documents, comes the ability to gain access to an international crime network. Unlike previous immigrants, who remained ghettoized for long periods of time in their new, different land, new immigrant populations benefit from the easy mobility in both legal and illegal fashions. Both entry into this country and exit from it can be achieved by this immigrant population without having to resort to the kinds of devious travel arrangements that were part of movement within their homeland.

Sources speculate that the drug traffic network that exists within the Soviet Union extends now, with the release of a new immigrant population, to outside of that country. This kind of crime, together with internationalization of money laundering and other international paper crimes, changes forever theoretical sociological understandings about immigrant crime of the past.

Of interest also, and different from those immigrants of the past, is the nature of the political arena. Previous immigrations left behind a homeland that had become unattractive for economic or social reasons. They moved to a land where they hoped they could make for themselves and for their children a new beginning. In a world where disruption has become part of the political arsenal, the new immigrants often still have questionable ties to the land from whence they came. It is hard to determine who left their homeland, because they were told to for governmental purposes. All my Russian informants, agreed that there was a segment among the new immigrants who had been sent here with Soviet governmental ties. These informants, who have grown up within a system where there is an understanding concerning being watched and watching, are particularly sensitive to this issue. It is hard to determine whether they continue to be spies, because they are so used to living with them that to be without them takes away some of life's importance, or whether indeed they are more perceptive concerning this particular aspect of world affairs.

Adding to the problem of definition in this area is the fact that American law enforcement agencies are hampered by lack of knowledge of the language. Consider that, until recently, on the newsstands in Brighton Beach was a small mimeographed newspaper entitled *The Spies Among Us* listing for all who read Russian the names of those who were known, while in the Soviet Union, to have ties to surveillance arms of the government. Yet, the New York City Police Department has virtually no Russian-speaking detectives but, for information, relies instead on the generosity of strangers.

Americans tend to regard the internationalization of crime and the specific arena of political disruption and crimes aimed toward the disturbance of an existing culture (i.e. the planned delivery of drugs into a society) as a right-wing area too absurd to discuss within scholarly circles. This may indeed prove to be the case, but again, it may not. In any case, this new immigration suggests that there are new kinds of research needed in areas that are, at this stage, highly speculative. Surely, the boundaries between local, national and international crime has blurred and the theoretical approaches to the study of the criminality of the immigrant must reflect this. At present, it appears difficult for police spokesmen to differentiate between people who have come here and continue to engage in criminal activities similar in nature or elaboration to those activities in which they engaged while in the Soviet Union, and those who have come here and maintain ties not only to criminals within various European cities but also to those within the Soviet Union with whom they dealt before immigration.

Implications

It is my conclusion that it is not the person who immigrates who changes his understanding, behavior and actions as a result of immigration but, rather, he brings with him his own moral code, developed in a faraway land, with which to analyze situations here. In some instances, his codes mesh with those of the surrounding society and in some they do not. Those who were engaged in behavior which, although criminal, was of utmost necessity for day-to-day survival, those that in this study are called the survivors, continue to utilize just as much extra legal behavior as needed for survival in their new land. Since much of their behavior there was not such as to be considered criminal here, these people may ultimately move out of their criminality into legitimate endeavors. They still maintain those skills and understandings with which they came armed, but their need for them may lessen in time. If they succeed in their new "legality," they may become socialized to American patterns of legality and illegality (white-collar crime). It is likely that such a transformation of consciousness may take more than one generation.

On the other hand, those whose existence within the Soviet Union was totally extra legal, whose interest in criminality was beyond that needed to support their family or their place at work, will also continue their illegal behavior upon immigration. These people referred to in this study as the connivers, were engaged in trades and business which are continued after immigration in criminal activities of the same sort as they were engaged in Russia. Burglary, arson, and fencing of goods continue to occupy their time, and their contacts continue to be with those who are and were engaged in similar pursuits. Additionally, with the ease of travel, the open state of borders, the "naivete" of agents of government, the conniver is able not only to continue but to excel in his criminal career. He manipulates papers, moves currency (both real and counterfeit), deals in credit and credit cards, and generally has at his disposal a wide avenue of illegal pursuits, unhampered as of yet by powerful governmental interference. It is the conclusion of this study that the behavior of the new Russian immigrant and his criminality (the exceptions noted) does not change upon immigration but, rather, that it is the public interpretation of this behavior which views it as legal or illegal that governs the criminality of the new Russian immigrant.

Further research is required, for this is indeed a large area for study. This model of the new immigrant can be viewed as having implications applicable to other new immigrant groups. The behavior of, for example, Haitians, Carribeans, Columbians, Dominicans, Koreans, Japanese, Chinese and Cubans, as well as internal migrants such as American blacks and Puerto Ricans, with respect to beating the system, paper manipulation, travel illegality and the working of multi-jurisdictions must be researched from the perspective of bureaucratically and industrially schooled populations whose immigrations are unlike those of previous peasant populations and for whom previous theories of immigrant criminality are insufficient. Additionally needed is research into the ways that these new immigrant populations are refurbishing already existing older criminal organizations or enterprises.

With the ease of travel, the ability to manipulate international markets and currency, diamonds and drugs, it is suggested that the day of studying criminality within only one jurisdiction is over. The criminal versed in world travel and skilled in movement, as is the sophisticated new Russian criminal, has already made his presence known through international crime upon international law enforcement contacts. The extent and degree of organization of such criminal activities cannot as yet be fully assessed. More time, more development and much more research will be necessary to assess this latter area. Lastly, it is of interest to discover how some people are able to maintain their own personal value system, their own state of morality while living in a society where every current moves them further toward some kind of criminal behavior, for they disprove all theory.

REFERENCES

Bell, D. Crime as an American way of life. *Antiocti Review*, *13*(June):131-154, 1953.
Ianni, F. A. J. *Black Mafia*. New York: Simon and Schuster, 1974.

INDEX

117